One Green Beret

# Contents

Chapter 1. Joint Commissioned Observer, Bihać, Bosnia
Chapter 2. Joint Commissioned Observer, Brčko, Bosnia
Chapter 3. Russian Liaison Team, Kamenica, Kosovo
Chapter 4. From after Kosovo to Iraq
Chapter 5. Advanced Force Operations
Chapter 6. Ugly Baby to Operation Viking Hammer
Chapter 7. Operation Viking Hammer
Chapter 8. The Green Line
Chapter 9. Geospatial Analysis and Intelligence Instructor
Chapter 10. Inter-agency Task Force
Chapter 11. Now

*This book is dedicated to my wife, my family, and the men of ODA-081, circa 2003*

*This book was approved by the DoD Prepublication Review Process*

*3$^{Rd}$ Edition, Dec 2021*

# Chapter 1
## Bihać, Bosnia, 1997-98
## Joint Commissioned Observer

In the early 1990s, Yugoslavia dissolved, and its various republics became independent. It started with Slovenia declaring independence, then Croatia, and soon after that, Bosnia and Herzegovina plunged into one of the most horrific civil wars in history. Inside Bosnia, the Croats (Catholic), Serbs (Orthodox), and Bosniaks (Muslims) fought each other viciously for territory (it wasn't so much over religion). Croats fought Bosniaks and Serbs. Serbs fought Bosniaks and Croats. Bosniaks and Croats teamed up to fight the Serbs. Mass expulsion and killing ensued, including the infamous Srebrenica massacre, as well as the mass expulsion of ethnic Serbs from Croatia (from an area known as Serbian Krajina). Criminal rogue elements capitalized on the chaos, and women were subjected to cruelty as law and order, and accountability, completely disappeared. In 1995, the Croats made a huge final push called Operation Storm, the Dayton peace accords were signed, and Bosnia was left with two entities whose territories are currently intertwined quite awkwardly. The two entities were the "Federation," which was a joint Bosniak and Croat entity, the second was the Serbian entity called the Republika Srpska (RS). Generally speaking, the US supported the Bosnian Muslims and the Croats during the war. As of 2021, the ethnic strife seems to be rising again, with secession of the RS becoming more and more likely.

After the war ended, peacekeeping forces (a new concept at the time) from many countries moved into various places all over Bosnia, and established bases. One of the most interesting concepts introduced was the Joint Commissioned Observer (JCO) missions. The JCO mission was to report "the pulse of the people" and they initially consisted of British special troops, but then transitioned to US Special Operations Forces. The purpose was to provide large scale situational awareness at the village level. Green Beret teams and SEAL teams lived together in rental houses in local communities all over the country as part of the JCO Mission.

It was 1997, I was 24 years old, and it hadn't been long since I had graduated high school, watched Panama and Desert Storm happen on the news, joined the Army, and completed 5 years as an Army infantryman. The last thing on my mind when my wife and I were driving from Fort Bragg, North Carolina to Fort Carson, Colorado was anything related to the establishment of a normal domestic life. I had no concept of looking for the perfect apartment or house, visions of quaint picket fences could not have been further from my mind, and I had not thought for a second about settling down to have kids in Colorado Springs. I was not at all behaving like a normal newlywed husband as we drove away to start a life together; but it wasn't because I didn't love my amazing Dominican wife that I had fallen in love with on a firing range in Ft Benning a year or so prior. It was because I had just successfully completed the Green Beret's "Special Forces Qualification Course."

I was dying to go off to a glorious war with my brand new Green Beret in my pocket, kind of like a new NFL player might dream of the super bowl. I had been informed in the final weeks of German language school -the final stage in Special Forces training in 1997- that I would be stationed in Colorado at the 10$^{th}$ Special Forces Group, and my unit was leaving for Bihać, Bosnia to perform the JCO mission.

Once I arrived at 10$^{th}$ Group and settled into my Operational Detachment Alpha (ODA) in Bravo Company, 3$^{Rd}$ Battalion (ODA 081), we started our "Pre-Mission Training," which was tailored to the JCO mission. Most training revolved around utilizing concealed pistols, since we'd be carrying only our 9MMs in concealed holsters. We ran through restaurant and riot scenarios, as well as situations like car jackings and roadblocks. After a few weeks of drills and flat-range pistol shooting, I remember kissing my wife goodbye and heading to the Team Room. We packed up, shipped out on military aircraft, stopped in Germany, and eventually landed in Sarajevo.

From Sarajevo, we drove SUVs westward across the country to Bihać on a cold and foggy morning. The conventional Army in Sarajevo looked at us in disbelief from under their helmets and body armor as we drove out of the gates in civilian vehicles with seemingly no weapons nor body armor, no headgear, as well as no patches or rank.

Bosnia reminded me of rural eastern Connecticut where I was raised, except for obvious architectural style differences. As we drove, I observed the small villages full of concrete block houses with red tile roofs that dotted the rolling hills along the windy narrow roads. It would have been immensely beautiful but most of the buildings had no windows, there were signs indicating land mines everywhere, and half of the buildings had been destroyed and reduced to piles of concrete shards. The others in the vehicle with me, the old-timers, were acting as if they were on a relatively normal ride. For me, this was my first deployment, so I was on pins and needles.

We arrived at our house in Bihać, a predominantly Muslim town, after an entire day of driving. The house was one of the biggest and nicest houses in the neighborhood. The house had three stories and a balcony, and there was a small liquor store at the end of our side street. People were sweeping the street outside of their houses and some waved to us as we drove in.

Bihać was a fairly typical European small town except for the scars of war that some of the buildings still bore; it had been under siege for an extreme amount of time. Bihać had narrow streets, mostly white concrete or stone buildings, small shops, and a slight smell of sewage when the wind was right. I was given my own room in the bottom floor of the house and my guitar was the first thing I unpacked. I'd played the guitar for my entire life, and I couldn't do without it for very long so I always brought it with me. I discovered soon enough that we were renting the place from a German couple. There was already half of a Navy SEAL team there that we would be working with the whole time as one team.

Since I was new to Special Forces, the lowest ranking Sergeant on the team, I was partnered with the senior Non-Commissioned Officer (NCO) from the SEAL team. As JCOs we were allowed to travel the country freely, driving SUVs, as two-man teams, with nothing but concealed pistols and a radio.

The SEAL explained to me our day to day mission, which was to talk to people, and report the situation across our sector. It was that simple. You could say that JCOing was the peacekeeping version of Zonal Reconnaissance. Our job was to meet with local politicians, Military, law enforcement, and regular citizens and simply report the situation to relay "the pulse" of our area of responsibility directly to the highest levels. I was a little disappointed when I realized we had little chance of seeing any combat. However, in hindsight, this would be one of the most interesting missions I did as a Green Beret, because of the cultural experience.

A day in the life of a JCO was to wake up in the morning, walk down the street to the bakery, buy some amazing warm bread that the baker always had waiting for us, then go back to the house where our cook made chocolate or fruit filled crepes called palachinkas. We would eat breakfast, and drink Turkish style coffee while we waited for the interpreters to show up so we could drive to our meetings for the day. We would then drive as two man teams to our sectors and meet with people. Some meetings with officials were scheduled, but we also frequently just stopped and spoke with random citizens at their houses or in small shops or restaurants. We would then return to the house, then write and submit our report for the day. We were nowhere near a US base, and we lived completely "on the local economy," which meant we lived exactly as the normal people that surrounded us did. In SF we call this "going native," and this was the modern sense of the phrase.

I fondly remember driving out of the house and over the stone bridge that crossed the Una River, and how beautiful the emerald green water was. I quickly learned that the beauty of Bosnia, land and people, was in stark contrast to the horrors of the war that had recently ended there. I learned about this war by traveling freely and talking to hundreds of random citizens and officials firsthand. One of our interpreters had been a victim of one of the rape camps that had been set up during the war. She never said much.

One day, my SEAL teammate and I, along with one of our interpreters, journeyed towards the town of Sanski Most in order to meet with one of the Bosniak military leaders in the area. Geographically, Sanski Most is just west of Tuzla, and north of a small town called Kluć. It was quite a drive from Bihać, it took us several hours to get there because of snow on the road that goes through Bosanski Petrovac. We decided to stop just south of Sanski Most to have lunch at a typical small-town chivapi joint. Chivapi is a traditional Bosnian food, and consists of small sausages on puffy flat bread. We sat down and ordered a chivapi and a coke. The restaurant was no bigger than 150 feet square, with maybe three or four crude wooden tables and a rough concrete floor, and it smelled very nice, like chivapi.

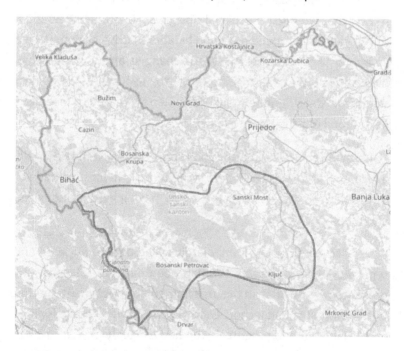

*My sector approximately (Map source: OpenStreetMap)*

A tall and muscular black man who wore dark blue jeans and a black jacket walked into the restaurant, looking extremely out of place for Bosnia, and as soon as he saw us he let out a sigh, the kind of sigh you let out when you've been casually discovered and feel obligated to explain yourself. He walked over and stood next to our table. He peered at us inquisitively for a second through his black rimmed glasses and smiled; he had stubble. My partner seemed a bit alarmed, and I assumed he was a member of some local NGO. Then he spoke in perfect American English,

"let me guess, a SEAL and a Green Beret?"

This was an amazing deduction, because as JCOs we didn't wear any patches, badges, or rank, so this man was able to deduce, simply based on our sewn-on labels US NAVY and US ARMY, that we must be special ops guys. He probably assumed this because only spec ops would be able to drive around Bosnia as only a two-person team. We exchanged a few of the usual pleasantries that strangers tend to exchange. The most significant statement he made was when he turned to face us as he stepped out the door to leave

"whatever they tell you after you report this, trust me I'm really a nice guy, in fact I am going to write a book about it someday." With that, he walked out the door, having never purchased anything.

My SEAL leader immediately called back to our base and reported what we'd seen. We had been directed to report any presence of foreigners in the area immediately. It turned out that this man we just had a short chat with was a well-known fugitive and "Islamic freedom fighter" who had allegedly played a role in the Beirut bombings against the Marine barracks in Lebanon during the 80s. When I heard this, I became enraged. The SEAL and I swore that if we saw him again, we were going to take it upon ourselves to kill him. As we drove towards the Bosniak General's Headquarters building for our scheduled meeting we talked about how easy it would be to get away with killing him in a place like Bosnia at that time.

The Bosniak General in Sanski Most was one of the most war hardened people I have ever seen (he was the General in charge of 5th Corps, Bosnian Army). He was missing a hand if I remember correctly, his face was heavily scarred and wrinkled, and his chest was full of medals. I admired him because he reminded me of my father, who had been severely wounded in Vietnam. Like my father, despite his rough appearance, he had a very kind and welcoming demeanor. We started the meeting with casual discussion, and one of the General's staff brought us all rakija to drink.

Rakija, also called slivovitz, is a sort of Bosnian moonshine, made from plums, and it is a cultural phenomenon in Bosnia. Bosniaks, Serbs, and Croats were very creative about how they made it and everyone from village to village crafted it their own special way. I grew to love tasting the different varieties. It was customary, regardless of whether I was meeting a Serb, Croat, or Bosniak, to drink lots of rakija. However, in my opinion, the Serbs produced the best stuff.

Most conversations in these meetings gravitated towards describing the unimaginable violence that had occurred in Bosnia, and it didn't take me long to realize that most normal people really couldn't explain how or why the war ever started. During this conversation with the General, we casually eased our way into asking if he had ever seen a large black American man in the vicinity. He started smiling excitingly as if he couldn't wait to tell us. He said, of course he'd seen him, everyone knew the American, he was a local war hero for fighting the Serbian and Croatian military and militia during the war. Of course, I was stunned at what he said. We ended the meeting on a good note and headed back to Bihać.

We didn't travel to Sanski Most more than two or three more times in the next five months, and we never saw the expat terrorist American again... I don't know if his book ever hit the shelves. The American was likely part of the Mujahedeen that came from various countries and operated in Bosnia on the side of the Muslims.

A month or so later, in a nearby village we reported on the exhumation of a mass grave of what was believed to be Serbian bodies near Kluć (one of many areas where the Croats and Bosniaks had pushed the Serbs out of Western Bosnia). All the bodies had been decapitated and thrown into a shallow ditch. All the heads of the dead had been piled into a nearby stone well a few dozen meters away. Some of the heads still had skin and hair, so I could still perceive their distorted human faces. Someone discovered that there were also more bodies than heads so we all tried to account for why that was the case, and I helped search the nearby area for the missing head. Being a hick from Eastern Connecticut, I assumed an animal of some kind had dragged one away somewhere. One of the NGOs told me that these beheadings were typical of the mujahedeen who had come to Bosnia to fight on the Muslim/Bosniak side. Many of the bodies also still had rope around their rotting wrists because their hands had been tied together behind their backs. I wondered if the local ex-pat American terrorist war hero had been involved in this specific incident. The smell of the scene was unforgettable, a combination of wet earth and old rotting remains; like a nasty roadkill near a freshly mowed lawn.

## One Green Beret

Most people think that the Serbs were to blame for everything that went wrong in the Balkans, but this event, and many others, taught me that the Serbian people were victims just like the others, and in some cases worse because the behavior of Serb politicians caused great consequences for the regular Serbian civilians. The Serbs always get pinned with "ethnic cleansing," but they were deliberately ethnically cleansed by Croats and Muslims from Croatia and Western Bosnia during Operation Storm in 1995 that left about a half million Serbs displaced. In my opinion, after hundreds of firsthand accounts of the war from people of all ethnicities, if you make the leap to charge the Serbs with ethnic cleansing, then it's only fair to charge the Croats and Bosniaks with the same.

Somewhere near the same area, we exhumed another mass grave in which there were bodies that had been executed with gunshot wounds to the back of the head, their hands had been tied, and pig carcasses had been thrown in the grave with them. It was believed that the grave contained Muslim people's bodies (hence the pigs as a way of desecrating the bodies), and it was guessed that the deeds were performed by militia of either Croatian or Serbian ethnicity, because in this area of Bosnia all three sides fought one another at different times.

I experienced similar horrors such as these the entire time we were in Bosnia, and I heard countless stories from hundreds of people that were much worse. Most of the killing was done as a vicious cycle of revenge, in which each iteration of the cycle caused the proverbial bar of savagery to be raised higher and higher. During WW2, the Croats were a Nazi puppet state called the Independent state of Croatia, and all the Serbs I met told stories of the Jasenovac Ustashe death camp, in which hundreds of thousands of Serbs and other groups were killed (reported numbers vary by source). The Croats were so brutal that it was said that even the German SS had to keep them under wraps. The Serbs and Croats have a terrible history that politicians on all sides exploited to sow fear, and fear has a way of generating unimaginable savagery.

We continued to meet and build rapport with dozens of great people, I drank gallons of rakija with them, and I listened intently to hundreds of unthinkable stories similar to the heads in the well from all walks of life across all ethnicities. In stark contrast to the horrors of the war, such as stories of rape camps and mass executions, I also experienced the friendliest and most genuine people I have ever met in my life.

One such experience took place continuously during this trip to Bosnia in a beautiful mountain village called Martin Brod. Martin Brod was a mostly Croat village south of Bihać, nestled in a valley along the banks of the emerald Una river with amazing waterfalls and a very interesting old stone church. Prior to the war, the border was actually west of the river, and to the west of the river there were better roads to get to civilization within what is now Croatia. The redrawn post-war border essentially split the village in two, and those left on the east side were declared Bosnian and the west Croatian, now separate countries, despite the fact that both sides were populated with people of mostly Croatian ethnicity. During the winter, people on the Bosnia side could not get out of the valley to go east for supplies due to heavy snowfall. Also, since there was a Croatian military machine gun position on the small bridge that led west into Croatia, people could not just cross over because this was now an international border. In one case, someone's elderly mother had died on the Bosnian side because her children in Croatia had not been allowed to cross over and take care of her. Due to the isolation,

## One Green Beret

people were suffering on the east side, and I became friends with some of them and I will never forget them.

His name was Pavle, or at least that's what we called him. He and his wife lived at the base of the beautiful waterfalls near a fish hatchery. Pavle was very thin, wore a moustache, was in his sixties I guessed, and had very typical Croatian features that I was used to seeing – sandy grayish hair, a fairly large pointed nose, and keen steel blue eyes. My partner and I would always bring Pavle and his village sacks of potatoes, and other goodies, that we would take from the Canadian base that was in our sector. Word spread in the village of our good deeds and we were soon introduced to many of the people in the village. Pavle always rolled out his best bread and rakija for us every time we visited, and we'd talk for hours. On our first trip to his house, we had both become so intoxicated on Pavle's exquisite rakiya while delving into deep conversations about the war, that after we departed his house we had to stop along the desolate snowy pass that led to Bihać and wait to sober up a little before continuing on.

I remember that Pavle frequently lamented about the loss of his son in the war. His son was a member of the Croatian army (HVO) and was killed in a battle somewhere north during the large operation that pushed the Serbs out of Croatia and parts of western Bosnia into what is now the Republika Srpska. Pavle hated the fact that he could not explain why the war ever happened, which made the loss of his son even more unbearable and seemingly senseless to him. He blamed the politicians and the media arms that aligned with each.

Pavle introduced us to an older couple that lived way up the steep hill from his house. Their house was nestled into the woods very close to the waterfalls; in fact, if the wind was right while we were sitting outside in the front of the house in lawn chairs, we could feel a light mist from the waterfall's vapor. Like Pavle's, the house was concrete block, whitewash color, with the quintessential red cupped tile roof nestled into a hardwood forest. It's all a bit fuzzy in my memory, but it seems to me now as very quaint, and reminded me in some ways of the small Connecticut colonial homes I grew up around. The first time we went there they asked if we wanted some coffee, and we said yes. We didn't realize that the couple had no electricity. The man's wife started the wood stove, boiled the water, ground some coffee beans, and she kindly delivered our coffee about two hours later. We graciously thanked her, and by the time the coffee was ready we were almost drunk on the man's interesting form of rakija, of which he was quite proud of due to its almost purple color created by the creative addition of mulberry. After drinking coffee, the man showed us his ingenious devices for running different machines using the power of the beautiful emerald waterfalls.

He had built a sophisticated wooden aqueduct mechanism that channeled water into his barn to run different machines, and into a 3 or 4 feet wide basket that was in a small side pool in the river. He showed us how inside the barn, he was able to power a grinding stone, and a sort of band-saw by opening the appropriate channel in the maze of small aqueducts he had built. Since I was raised in rural Connecticut, grandson of a cabinet maker, and a woodworker myself, it was the underwater basket that intrigued me the most because I could not figure out what it was.

The man smiled from ear to ear when I admitted my inability to deduce the basket's purpose. He took obvious enjoyment, as his sparsely-toothed grin indicated, at the fact that he had stumped the friendly young American. He went to fetch some items of clothing from the house, which made no sense to me. He put the cloths into the water, then used a stick that was part of this basket's componentry to push the clothes down into the basket with the stick and put a lid on it so the cloths would stay under water; the lid had a simple locking mechanism. He then opened up a channel in the aqueduct system that fed water towards the outer edge of the basket. The sudden and continuous rush of water violently tumbled the cloths in a circular fashion. Alas! it was clothes washing machine. He said he would let it run for a while and then hang the clothes out to dry. It was awesome, and it reminded me of the many jigs my grandfather had fashioned for tapering bedposts and accomplishing other woodworking feats. In these rural parts of Bosnia, I felt very comfortable.

These people were living like pioneers, and their unbelievable hospitality, toothless grins, homemade bread, grainy coffee, creative rakija, and general human spirit again made me wonder how did war ever happen in Bosnia? These people claimed that it seemed like one day they were friends and neighbors with Bosniaks and Serbs, but the next they were all trying to kill each other and doing horrible things to each other. It was as if some invisible force had compelled or commanded them to do so, and no one I ever spoke to in Bosnia could explain the source of this propulsion, other than politicians and their biased media. Like these people in this village, there were hundreds of other tiny, and amazing, villages of some of the most peaceful people I had ever imagined, all somehow thrust into feeling like they had to do violence to one another but none could explain why.

Despite what the news had reported, I had come to the realization that it was impossible to nominate any particular ethnicity as "the bad guys" in Bosnia. The Serbs were not evil. The Croats were not saints. The Bosniaks were not the only victims. All civilians of all ethnicities were the true victims of this war. The politicians and their media lackies should be ashamed of themselves for what happened in Bosnia. Now it's 2021, and I wish the leaders of my country and their media lackies would learn from what happened in Bosnia, but I have a feeling they won't.

A new team arrived to replace us after about six months, I showed them around and introduced them to all the great people I met with; the Serbian owner of the "end of the world café" in Kluć, Pavle and his wife and our waterfall friends, the Bihać soccer team, the guy who spoke German that I went fishing with on a stream that was lined with landmines, the General in Sanski Most, the Serb police outside of Banja Luka, and many more. They were all people just like us, just trying to live through an unimaginable set of circumstances. When we said our goodbyes to Pavle we grew emotional, and then the Croatian checkpoint almost shot us that day because one of the guards was drunk. I won't forget Pavle waving in the rear-view mirror with the Croatian mountains behind him. I have a picture of Pavle that I occasionally look at and smile, thinking about sitting in his small living room, and I can still taste the rakiya. I wish I could go back someday and see if he's still there, but it was 20 years ago now. I always wanted to bring him a bottle of wine or Jack Daniels to repay him for all the rakiya he gave us. Leaving Bosnia had a similar feeling to when I left my childhood home to go to boot camp. Bosnia is a powerful place, it is a big part of who I am, and I will never forget it.

## One Green Beret

Although I didn't describe every detail of my trip, here is a stream of consciousness that expresses some other interesting memories ... the Bihać municipal soccer team – I played on it, the drunk guy who gave us free beer at the end of our street, ordering pizza *bez jajas* (without cracked eggs on top), fishing with the guy who spoke German on the Una river, the priests in Martin Brod that we got hammered with along with some NGOs, the Croatian border guards at the top of Mount Gora didn't seem to like us being there – we crashed the car and almost died driving back down, the old Yugoslav airbase that was inside the mountain in Bihać and filled with landmines, the fact that none of the Muslims in Bihać wore robes and rode camels or had scimitars or wanted to cut my head off, the Serbian police who wore purple uniforms and liked to drink with us and dispel myths about the Serbs, Ramadan in Bihać – a big party where 16 people were wounded by celebratory small arms fire, the bridges over the waterfalls in Martin Brod, the National park in Croatia that was amazing, trips to Zagreb to get our mail, driving through destroyed villages everywhere, chivapi in Karlovac on the way to Zagreb, the Serb police that couldn't decide whether to kill us or get drunk with us –they chose the latter and then many man-hugs ensued, and the list of unforgettable experiences with these great people goes on and on.

As we drove back to Sarajevo to leave the country and we passed through the razor wire encircled gates of the base where the US conventional Army stood diligently and sternly on guard in full body armor behind machine guns, I chuckled thinking that none of that "battle rattle" was necessary. I knew firsthand that the last thing anyone in Bosnia wanted to see was more warfare that was created by politicians who never really represented them. Bosnia taught me a lot about war.

Although this deployment wasn't full of sexy Spec-Ops black helicopters, it taught me how different Green Berets are compared to conventional forces and other SOF (SEALs stopped doing the JCO mission – it was not a good fit). The idea of an E5 and an E7 driving around in an SUV with an interpreter, anywhere they wanted, anytime they wanted, for any reason they came up with, wearing no rank, no patches, and only carrying a concealed pistol, would be considered totally insane in the conventional military. Moreover, our reports went straight to the highest levels, so our reporting was trusted. This trip was my first Special Forces experience, and one that I cherish greatly as I age.

During this whole trip, my wife and I, newlyweds and very young, wrote letters back and forth intermittently, some of which I tried to write in Spanish. My wife was back home doing her thing, alone, teaching Spanish in Colorado Springs and thinking about getting her Masters degree.

One Green Beret

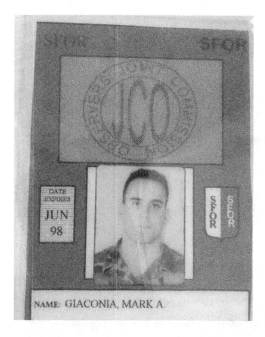

*My JCO ID Card*

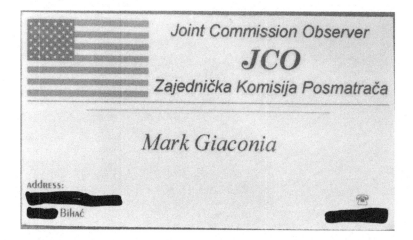

*My JCO Business Card*

*Pavle and his wife in their house in Martin Brod, with my Team Sergeant and I (the date on the image is wrong, photo is mine)*

## Chapter 2
### Brčko, Bosnia, 1999
### Joint Commissioned Observer

This time It was 1999, NATO was on the verge of war with Serbia due to the war in Kosovo, and we were about to live in a house in Brčko, a very important mostly Serb town (at that time) in a district that essentially splits Bosnia's Republic of Serbia at its northern chokepoint.

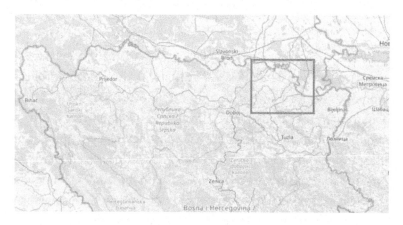

*My sector approximately (Map source: OpenStreetMap)*

Again, we lived in a rental house, but this one was not nearly as nice as our house in Bihać. The house was located on the southern side of the city, only about 100 meters north of the train tracks that cross the Sava river into Croatia. When we entered the house, it had a totally different aura than Bihać; to me it had an aura of war. Every window had sandbags in front of it, hence creating a sort of bunker out of every window. There was chicken wire on all the windows – to keep grenades and maltove cocktails from being thrown into the house. I was kind of excited about the potential for combat as I walked around and examined the sandbag reinforced house. Again, one of the first things I unloaded and set up in my room was my guitar, and this time I had brought my electric guitar.

The other Green Beret team that we were there to replace was completely convinced that the Serbian locals, and possibly the Bosnian Serb military, were going to attack the house at any second. Because of this assumption, the house was like living permanently in a bomb shelter awaiting imminent attack. The wisdom I had gained in Bihać made me doubt the validity of this notion that we were facing imminent danger from the Serbs.

The team we were replacing was adamant about being ready to occupy several key positions in the house within a moment's notice in order to fend off a hostile attack. They had acquired an armored Humvee from our headquarters in Tuzla and kept it hidden in the garage so that they had an emergency escape vehicle. They had coordinated a quick reaction force, referred to as a QRF, as a rescue team, with the American brigade that was stationed in the stronghold of Camp McGovern, which was on the outskirts of Brčko about 8 miles or so from our house. We did several rehearsals with them, which took quite a lot of painful coordination on our part. This is where I learned that the hardest part of any Special Operations mission is dealing with US conventional forces; dealing with an enemy typically pales in comparison in regard to complexity.

As an 18B (the Military Occupational Specialty (MOS) for a Special Forces Weapons Sergeant), I was responsible for physical security. So, as part of this responsibility, I routinely initiated rescue rehearsals by the use of a siren inside the house. I used a stopwatch to see how fast everyone would get to their positions, and how fast we were able to make communications with the QRF at camp McGovern. Everyone got up, got their combat gear on, and was in position in a superb amount of time, and we were able to talk to the QRF within a minute or so. The plan was that they would come to our house with a convoy of appropriate size (based on the situation as we described to them) and they said they were preparing to roll out of the gates.

We waited, and waited, and they finally showed up about an hour later, blundering down our street in armored vehicles, and we met them in the front yard with nothing but boxer shorts, boots, and body armor on. Actually, my Warrant Officer might have even been completely naked except for body armor and combat boots. Conventional military forces and Special Forces rarely see eye to eye, and the QRF leadership really didn't appreciate that we were not in proper uniform, although all the "Joes" thought we were awesome. Regardless, the point is that we were all so convinced that we were in imminent danger that we all took the time and expended the effort to coordinate this type of emergency exfiltration drill.

So we continued this way of life, locked in a sandbagged house, sort of like I imagined jail might be like, for almost a month, waiting for the inevitable start of war, and the consequences of that war. Our morale, our patience with each other, and our health, started to deteriorate.

Towards the end of March, NATO began bombing Serbia unmercifully. We listened to military radio transmissions from our operations room intently on most days so we could hear what others were reporting. There were many reports of Bosnian Serb riots in our town center; these riots were described as "violent anti American and anti-NATO" protests against the bombing of Serbia. Many people in Brčko had family in Belgrade and other parts of Serbia, and they were mourning the effects of the NATO airstrikes (which targeted both military and core infrastructure).

After the old team had been gone for a couple of weeks, an order came down from our headquarters that directed us to get out of the house and collect information, which meant that our company commander didn't think we were doing our jobs, which of course we weren't. This is one of the many times I felt like the leaders above me made a good call. I was the only person on my team that had done the JCO mission before (we had a lot of turnover between deployments), so I conferred with my Captain to help figure out how to proceed.

My Captain, like pretty much every other Special Forces officer I ever worked with, was very open minded and willing to listen to good ideas. The best I could come up with is that I thought we should look at a map, figure out where all the villages are, and go there to build rapport and talk to the local people, government, and law enforcement... all of which meant we had to actually *leave the house*, enter the world of the evil Serbs, and start JCO-ing like we had in Bihać.

We divided our sector into pieces and assigned two man teams to each sector. I was team leader for a sector that extended west about 30 miles and constituted a variety of Croat, and Serb towns along the Sava river (which separates Croatia from northern Bosnia.) We prepared and began patrolling the next morning. I became the de facto JCO-ing coach for the team.

Interestingly, I hadn't even spoken to our interpreter yet; I hadn't needed to because we had never gone anywhere. His name was Goran, and he was a Serbian combat veteran who had been wounded in battle somewhere near Orašje (a Croat pocket within northern Bosnia). My first patrol was to Bosanski Šamac, which according to intel was notorious for being a place filled with "hardline" Serbs. As we drove through Brčko headed towards Šamac, it was interesting to see that Brčko was a bit more run down than Bihać, but had quite a few similarities, such as the whitewashed buildings, and instead of mosques there were mostly orthodox Serb churches. It took us about 45 minutes or so to get there. As we drove, Goran pointed out the sites of old battles where he had fought and friends of his had died. He pointed out all the roads that "you never go down" if you're a Serb, and other assorted facts and opinions you might expect from a young Serb war veteran with blonde highlights in his hair and a fanny pack.

    He told us a story of how at one point there were so many dead bodies in the Sava river that it had actually caused a dam, and that his unit was charged to clear the river of bodies down near Brčko. He was obviously traumatized by the event of having to touch the mangled bodies, and remove them from the river (a story I would eventually relate to). He said the Croat HVO would tie people together with rope on the bridge that went from Orašje into Croatia, and then smash a few of the people in the head with sledge hammers, then kick them all off the bridge into the Sava. The dead ones with crushed skulls would weigh the others down and they would drown in the bloody water. He said that if any people somehow got free and tried to swim to safety they were shot. I have no idea if this actually happened, but it's what he said, and at the time it didn't seem like an unreasonable story given the history of barbarity throughout Bosnia. Since the Sava flows from west to east, apparently the bodies floated quite a distance downstream towards Brčko before enough of them accumulated in narrow areas. Of course this was speculation on our part; we speculated about horrid things like this all the time casually as we talked with various people about the unimaginable level of violence that had been achieved in Bosnia (such as human hunting safari escorts bringing people in from foreign countries so they could shoot random people for fun).

We continued past the Road that led to Orašje, through some rural countryside, and we arrived in Bosanski Šamac. It was a fairly run down small village with one main street, the only real features I remember were the mayor's office, a park like open area in the middle, and the World War Two Chetnik veterans building.

We parked our car at the end of the street near a patch of trees, got out and then started walking towards where the mayor's office was along the sidewalk. The small park-like area was across the road to my right, and I was a bit nervous. There weren't many people on the street, but there was a guy in a wheelchair that Goran had served in the Army with, who had had both legs blown off with an anti-aircraft machine gun while fighting the Croats. People looked at us as if they didn't know why we were there, but no one said anything at all, they just looked at us curiously (we were wearing "sterile" uniforms, no rank, no patches, no hats, and no visible weapons).

We entered the very plain, grey building where the mayor was, and his secretary shook my hand and brought us to a room to talk. The mayor was around forty, about five foot eight with dark hair and eyes. It was very tense when he walked in; he didn't know what to expect from two Americans; we were actively bombing Serbia at this time, and he was a Serb. He asked us if we wanted something to drink. My JCO instincts kicked in and I asked him if he had any fine rakija on hand; his face brightened, and he instantly smiled. We then began a long discussion about all the different types of rakija I had experienced in western Bosnia. Instant rapport was established as he tried to convince me that the Serbs make the best rakija.

It wasn't long before, in the usual JCO way, we were both intoxicated and talking about how ridiculous the war had been. He told us about how he didn't understand how the Serbian people got pegged as the bad guys, which was a theme that would repeat with everyone I spoke to in the area, including non-Serbs. The mayor admitted that the Serb Army and militias did some brutal things, but so did all the other factions. He also complained that all the NGO and NATO or EU money never went into reconstruction of Serb areas in Bosnia, including his town. Although he complained about it, he also proudly stated that the Serbs didn't need any help from anyone anyway, but it still annoyed him.

Soon any notions I had that the Serbs were evil melted away along with my sobriety, and we finally left the office and I stumbled out onto the street. As soon as I hit the sidewalk, an old man came out of nowhere and hugged me vigorously saying something excitedly in Serbian that I did not understand. Apparently, word had spread that some Americans were in town. I was surprised by the man's enthusiasm, and his demeanor was so obviously friendly I did not feel threatened. Goran explained to me that the man was a member of the Chetnik veterans group, and that the Chetniks loved Americans.

They were sad and perplexed that we were bombing Serbia after Serb Chetniks had saved American pilots during the Second World War (WWII). They were also adamant about the fact that the Croats were one of the most brutal Nazi puppet states during WWII, and they were disgusted with what the Croats "got away with" regarding the Krajina (Serbian enclaves in Croatia that the Croatians "ethnically cleansed" during the Bosnian wars). They loved to tell us about the horrific things the Croatian Ustasha did to Serbs and others during WWII as well as during the Bosnian wars.

Serbs have a very different sense of time than Americans do, to them WWII might as well have happened last week, and the same goes for the epic battle of Kosovo against the Turks, which I repetitively heard folklore about throughout my trip. Later in life I read more about the Croats during WW2, and I can see why the history of Croatian atrocities is very fresh in Serbian minds.

My dangerous excursion into the treacherous hardliner Serb enclave of Bosanski Šamac fully replenished my old JCO spirit, including the part of the spirit that contains frustration over the extreme lack of glorious warfare involved in the day to day life of a JCO. I continued to visit many people in Šamac; the Chief of Police, the Mayor, President of the Serbian Democratic Party, as well as the President of the Serbian Radical Party.

I had been a few weeks since NATO started bombing Serbia, and we received reports that radical factions of Serbs may become violent within Bosnia. I saw zero indication of this anywhere and we had become deeply interactive with the local Serbs. In fact, I found the Serbs to be generally much more hospitable than most Croats and Muslims during my previous trip to western Bosnia.

I instructed my interpreter to set up a meeting with the Serbian Radical Party (SRS) president in Šamac. Since the SRS was notoriously anti NATO and anti US, at first he refused to speak with us. During the previous meetings I had with other political entities, as well as meetings with NGOs and other locals, I had gained the perception that no one really took the SRS seriously because they spewed too much hyperbolic rhetoric. After several failed attempts, and having abandoned all the false senses of fear I entered the country with months before, one day we found the SRS office in Šamac and just walked in. Just to put this in perspective, we were American soldiers, in a Serbian town in 1999, visiting the Serbian Radical Party, at the same time one could hear US aircraft overhead on their way to bomb the hell out of Serbia. Needless to say, he became annoyed when we walked in, but since we were physically standing there, there was nothing he could do about it. He sat back in his chair grimacing with arms crossed.

I started out listening to him rant about how the Serbs were always blamed for everything in the war. He delivered exceptionally deep details and stories to articulate his position; very typical political Serbian rhetoric focused on Krajina and Kosovo. My genuine interest, humility, inquisitiveness, and questions about what happened in those places are probably what made him finally open up to me after he got everything off his chest. Most of what the SRS was concerned with centered on Kosovo (the reason we were bombing Serbia) and how absurd it was that NATO was going to give Kosovo away to the Albanian rebels, who, in his opinion, overran the province of Kosovo through decades of illegal immigration, filth, criminal activity, and ultimately terrorism. He made the analogy that if Europe was a pair of white underwear, the Albanians would be the shit stain.

I had experienced this sentiment towards Albanians when speaking to Croats on several occasions as well (and

Albanians are not well liked across many other parts of Europe either). The conversation took many turns, but somehow it ended up with me providing him with political advice based on inputs I had heard from the other competing political parties in the area. My unintentionally humble interaction apparently calmed him down, and he actually thanked me for this advice. My advice was really simple: stop barking counter-productive propaganda. Over time I earned his respect, and after several more visits we were drinking rakija and laughing just like all the other folks, even when opinions varied (I didn't have much of an opinion, I was a philosophical chameleon).

During another random visit with him, he articulated a particular analogy that stuck with me over all these years, designed to convince me that the US was a "child of a nation" in comparison to Yugoslavia, the history of the Serbs, Europe, and ultimately the world (something he liked to remind me of... I was a young man then).

The analogy was relevant to Kosovo, and it was probably my first formal lesson in relativism. His analogy of Kosovo was posed to me as a series of questions; a dialectic of sorts. It began something like this:

"What would you do If you were the POTUS, and over time cartels that have saturated Texas decided they were going to overthrow the government of Texas via creating an insurgent group, bombing and attacking police, and killing random people to claim independence?"

I said of course that I would take military action. His subtle head nod indicated that this was the answer he had expected.

He continued with another question.

"What would you do if when you started taking military action to take back your *own* state of Texas, China started disproportionally bombing Washington DC and NYC?"

I said something like I would tell China to go to hell. Again, this is the answer he expected. He continued.

"What would you do if your war tactics were scrutinized because of a lack of tactical precision, and media bias, but you lacked the technology to be any more precise about it?"

I didn't know what to say, because he was starting to push the boundaries of my then quite poor critical thinking skills. Soon the analogy and dialectic faded into another diatribe. He also asked me another question, in relation to the fact that the Serbs had been accused of genocide.

"Why wasn't the US accused of genocide during Vietnam, after all, the US was only killing Vietnamese people?"

I laughed and told him that we were killing Vietnamese people because that's the only kind of people we were fighting, and they were "the enemy." Of course, this was again the answer he expected.

"Why were the Serbs accused of genocide in Kosovo then? We were only killing Albanians, and Albanians were our declared enemy, so what was the difference?"

I said that it was because civilians were being targeted. He smiled and continued.

"In guerilla warfare, the only difference between a civilian and the enemy is whether or not they are shooting at you at any given time. The UCK was not a nation state Army, they were irregulars, insurgents, like the Viet Cong."

He went on to explain that several times the Serb Army fought the UCK, and afterwards the UCK would take the weapons off the bodies, to stage a scene that looked like civilians had been murdered on the news, although they had been fighters moments before.

Amazingly, most Serbs were sophisticated enough to differentiate us, the JCOs, from the politicians who decided to do the 1999 bombings. The SRS president and I essentially became friends, and I would often bring him Jack Daniels from the Orašje Duty Free shop and we would get hammered as he, as usual, taught me the hardline Serb party line, and explained the difference between what the US news reported and what the situation was like in reality. We also frequently debated the meaning of "genocide" in the context of whether or not what happened in Srebrenica truly qualified as genocide. In my opinion today, I think that the Srebrenica massacre was a war crime for sure, but since women and children, and noncombatants, were not exterminated, then it does not qualify as genocide.

One day in Brčko, there was a "potentially violent protest" in the town square according to radio traffic from some conventional unit that was on patrol. I convinced my team leader that we should go see what really goes on at these things, because I had a strange feeling that they weren't what they seem. So, we set out on foot from our house, the riots were right down the street about a half a mile or so, and in a few minutes I was approaching the outskirts of the Serb demonstration in the center of Brčko. The voices of the large crowd grew louder as I approached.

There were several thousand Serbs crammed into the town center, Serbian flags waved everywhere, a rippling sea of colors and murmuring people sprawled out for hundreds of yards before me. They had made large scarecrow mannequins of Bill Clinton and Madeline Albright, both of whom were smothered in red paint simulating blood and hanging from nooses above the crowd at the end of long sticks. They also creatively reenacted the Monica Lewinsky ordeal by simulating oral sex between the Bill Clinton scarecrow and a Monica Lewinsky scarecrow. I had to laugh at the sight of that; it was interesting how our president's behavior made it easy for them to claim we were a bunch of hypocrites and should not be judging any nation on moral grounds, which was exactly what we had done to the Serbs regarding Kosovo in their opinion.

As I walked slowly up to the edge of the impetuous crowd, some younger people on the edge noticed me, and started to look at me in disbelief. First, I thought they might attack me, but then I quickly realized that the looks in their eyes were not a look of violence or anger, but a look of *fear*: they were actually scared of me. Then I thought about this fear empathetically, and from the perspective of a young Serb, if the US would bomb Serbia into the stone age for attempting to defend their own country, why would they think that I, a US soldier, was *not* there to kill *them* for protesting it all?

I knew that how I presented myself to them would be very important to how they reacted, and if I sent the wrong signal I could be in very serious trouble. So I gave them a gentle wave and a laid back head nod, then ran my hand through my out-of-

One Green Beret

Army-regulation-length hair in an attempt to passively communicate that I meant no harm. Then I calmly put my hands in my pockets, casually looked around, and hoped that my instincts about people were right.

So there I was, a long haired US soldier, weaponless, hands in my pockets looking casually and inquisitively into a crowd of about a thousand Serbs that were protesting against the ongoing US and NATO bombings of Serbia, in a mostly Serb town, in Bosnia.

A few people neared me and shouted *"Fuck Bill Clinton!"* or *"Albright is a murdering Babushka"* and other humorous anecdotes. A few dozen people, some of who spoke some English, came closer and started saying they hate Bill Clinton and they hate the US…. I responded in English but they did not fully understand, so Goran translated and told them I said "yeah, I can't say I blame you guys."

Once they knew I said this, their faces relaxed in surprise, the tenuousness diminished, and the word spread like fire in the wind through the few hundred people who were on the edge of the crowd near where I was standing. Within a few minutes, the fear in their eyes completely faded, I shook a few hands, and after appearing more and more approachable, I was having a conversation with a dozen or so people, mostly young people. One of the core competencies in SF is the ability to build rapport, and sometimes it's a matter of physical security.

After a few more minutes of chat, I ascertained that the main reason people came to these "riots" was because it was the only interesting thing for people to do. They explained that since there was no economy anymore because the war had destroyed the country's infrastructure, especially in Serb areas, and therefore no one had jobs, everyone came to the protests to hang out with their friends out of sheer boredom. Sure, they were mad about NATO killing their brethren, but they weren't violent animals. These people had just barely survived one war they never wanted, and now they were being impacted by yet another (and as Serbs they were blamed for both). Once I got personal with them, they quickly differentiated me from the politics, theirs and ours, that made it all happen.

As I spoke to the people on the edge of the "riot" I used my radio to talk to the conventional troops that were poised to swoop in and rescue us from the violent Serb protesters, and I told them that there was nothing to fear. Watching me tell the conventional troops that there was nothing to fear made the people around me very happy; it was as if they wanted me to trust them. A common theme among Serb people was that they were looking for someone to see their side of the story, to understand that normal Serbian people were victims of the Bosnian war just like the innocent people of the other ethnicities.

From this time on, we were welcome regulars at the anti US protests. One time we sat on lawn chairs on the outskirts of the riots and drank slivovitz with the locals, with Goran always willing to explain to anyone how "cool" and pro Serb we were. In fact, on at least one occasion we helped him pick up girls. Similar to how a guy might use a cute puppy as an ice breaker prop, Goran used the Americans. We had become trusted– just by walking outside and talking to people.

I must say I grew quite partial to the Serbs during this trip, mainly because their amazing hospitality, honesty, and level of pride; they reminded me of Americans in many ways. However, I would be remiss to not describe the Croats I met with, and how really irrelevant the different ethnic labels were prior to the political propaganda that fueled the war.

We drove towards Orašje, a Croat pocket along the Croatian border, to meet with the Croat mayor there. On the way into what used to be enemy territory for Goran, he pointed out a destroyed village on the right and identified it as the place where he had been dragged, wounded severely by the Croats, and was picked up by his parents to embark on a journey to find a functional hospital. At first, I thought it was crazy that his parents picked him up in the middle of a war, but then I realized that this war happened in peoples' back yards, not in some faraway place. He pointed out where the Croat front lines used to be, and nervously described how fiercely the Croats fought.

Interestingly, as we drove up the road it was shockingly apparent how much more improved the conditions were in the Croat enclave than in the Serbian areas. There was a clean line in the road where new pavement started, and there was even a painted line down the center of the road. As we approached the bridge that went into Croatia, the Federation (Bosniak and Croat) military barracks became visible on the Right, Goran was very uneasy as we took a left to go into the center of Orašje. I parked the car and walked across the street to what amounted to the town hall building. As we walked through the door Goran was practicing his Croat accent for what he was going to ask. It reminded me of a time in Army Airborne School when a friend of mine from Alabama brought me to his hometown. My eastern Connecticut accent really stood out, and some of his family instantly and automatically disliked me because of it. I didn't have much of a plan at all for the Orašje mayor.

We walked through the door, and Goran told the receptionist that we had an appointment. She instantly asked if he was a Serb, he reluctantly said yes; I guessed he was not able to adapt his accent or dialect enough to trick her. I think it surprised him that she really didn't care, she was just curious, because she smiled. I think she took a liking to him a bit (he was quite a dashing young fellow I guess, highlighted hair with fannypack and all). Soon someone came down and took us upstairs. We sat in a fairly large board room with nice chairs and a big shiny wooden table.

The mayor was a small man with sandy colored hair, and he looked annoyed. He immediately said that he talks to dozens of people about the same things all the time and didn't understand what we could possibly talk about that day that was not already accounted for.

Since he didn't want to talk about the same old stuff, I simply told him neither did I. So, I told him what our JCO job was, and I asked him what he *did* want to talk about. I did my usual rapport building, asking all the right questions, and within an hour or so he saw me as someone different, and he told me about how much his wife hates his job. One thing I realized in Bosnia, and everywhere else I have ever been, is that a man can always build rapport with another man on the basis of how little they understand about the women in their lives; I'm sure the same is probably true for women. The mayor and I drank a significant amount of slivovitz and we enjoyed each other's company about once per week until I left Bosnia.

One day when leaving Orašje after a meeting with the Mayor, we headed west into a rural area within the Orašje Croat pocket very near to Šamac (the border of the RS and the

Federation). We stumbled upon what looked like a place that sold tombstones – which we joked about morbidly, proclaiming that such an enterprise might be a lucrative business in Bosnia during the 90s. There was also the very odd presence of Ostriches roaming around in the open. We stopped and a highly energetic mid-sized man in his 60s with a toothless smile approached us. He had messy grey hair, and halfway unbuttoned Hawaiian shirt that revealed his grey haired chest. He was ecstatic that someone from NATO came to the village, and he immediately invited us to his house, which was a short walk under the canopy of large trees surrounding the area where we had parked.

He gave us slivovitz of course, and he also gave us a very special meat pie. All this happened very fast, and I noticed that his sons, and many other people who had gathered due to our presence, were regarding the old man with almost a bit of reverence. So I asked the man what he used to do before the war. This is when he began to detail how he had been a Croat politician of some kind, and how the corruption during the war had driven him out of the business, and he basically ran off to the countryside with his family and became an Ostrich farmer.

He articulated, in such detail that it took me several visits with the old man to fully comprehend, a list of all the people on the Croatian side of the war who were war profiteers (in his opinion), and who were involved with the ethnic cleansing of Serbs from Croatia (Knin and the Krajina), and other random political mishaps that occurred during the war. One of the most important techniques in JCO-ing is information cross validation. So I never took anyone's word for anything point blank, I always weaved it into a conversation with a few more people to try to coax out the true veracity of the statements, since everyone has an agenda. This is where the Orašje Mayor comes back into the picture.

So once I felt like I had understood as many details as I could from the Ostrich farmer, my plan was to casually run the information past the Mayor and see what he said: cross validation. So, the next time I met with the Mayor of Orašje, I started asking questions regarding the connective tissue to what the ostrich farmer told me. I was probably a bit heavy handed about it, and he definitely caught on that someone had given me a lot of detailed information. He did not say much at the time, but about a week later he actually used the phone number on my JCO business card and called our house in Brčko, and he set up what Goran translated as a "secret meeting," on a boat-restaurant on the Sava River in Orašje. It was odd that the Mayor of a major Croat village would reach out, via a Serbian interpreter, to set up a special meeting with us.

*My JCO Business card*

So I drove there at night, and met the Mayor on the large dark boat. He had reserved the entire restaurant boat for privacy. There was an aura of mystery about the place as I walked in with

Goran, like an old mob movie or something; kind of stuffy, low light, a bit smoky, red velvet seats, close proximity, and the air was thick with earnest. The mayor and I both sipped rakiya and looked across the table curiously into each other's eyes with a degree of seriousness that initially shocked me. He described to me all the background connected to the questions I had asked him. It turned out that the main point of this secret meeting was that he wanted to educate me on the complexity of the situations he was in, and clear his name by clarifying much of what the - obviously biased- ostrich farmer had said.

Much of the "bad" things that we talked about were really minuscule political or military mishaps and poor decision making during chaotic times which he wasn't really involved in, but some things were fuzzily connected to larger issues. He also talked about local atrocities that had taken place, small incidents in terms of world news events, but had been life altering and significant emotional events to him. The Mayor convinced me that he was clean, and he wanted to make sure that what I reported had sufficient granularity and confidentiality. To be clear, he did not make any confessions, nor did he need to; he just further educated me on how complex the situation in Bosnia was, from a Croat's perspective.

He was really adamant about how confused everyone was that the war got to the point that it did, the way the violence spread and escalated, and how no one noticed how it was spiraling out of control until it was too late. Everyone in Bosnia was overwhelmed with the circumstances of a war they never wanted. After him and I exchanged man-hugs after this meeting, and I was subsequently crafting my report to our headquarters, I reflected on how touching it was that this man grew to trust me to such a degree, especially since experiences such as his make trust difficult to establish with anyone. This was one of those moments when I felt the enormity of what this horrific war in Bosnia had put these poor people through. The turmoil, chaos, death, corruption, and destruction around them during the war was something that I could not imagine, literally, and that intensity laced our conversation that day in the boat with a level of gravity that I had never before experienced in my life. I did a lot of growing up in Bosnia, and in hindsight my experiences now feel like a part of my childhood.

During one of my subsequent conversations with the ostrich farmer, he told us we should try to find a person in the area known as the "Spider." The Spider was allegedly an ex criminal war profiteer, who lived somewhere near Šamac, but just inside the Croat Orašje pocket.

I went to investigate by visiting the spider's restaurant. We walked in, took a seat in an air conditioned room, and asked the waiter if we could talk to the Spider. Soon enough he sat with us for lunch, a very normal looking man. He regretfully told us that he did some bad stuff during the war like everyone else, dispelled the rumor that he was involved in the smuggling of prostitutes into the area, but he did rat out a Serbian guy, presumably a competitor during his criminal years. So that's where we went next.

We turned off the main road and then rounded a corner and saw an extremely large, and therefore out of place, three story house nestled into a dirt cul de sac surrounded by trees. This house was huge, like an American McMansion, a complete anomaly in Bosnia. We parked the car and walked to the door. I knocked loudly, and then heard a subtle commotion that indicated someone was coming to the door. I grew a bit uneasy, and I was ready to go for my concealed pistol when a short plump woman gently opened the door smiling. I said hi in Serbo Croatian, and asked if I could speak to the man we were looking for. She let us in, and led us up three flights of stairs. As the son and grandson of talented New England craftsmen, I immediately noticed that there was beautiful woodwork everywhere in the house; mainly consisting of very intricate lathe work in the staircase in what looked like mostly chestnut, which had been perfectly finished in a honey stain and very nice varnish. There was also no furniture on the first floor at all.

We arrived in a large room with very little furniture, with a few children playing on the floor and another woman there. A very sickly looking little man with very few good teeth stood up and welcomed us to his house. We asked the man about what the Spider had said, he confirmed that he was the guy we were looking for, and that he had indeed done some not-so-great stuff during the war. He was now a family man, owned a few gas stations that didn't make much money, and he really just wanted to be left alone. He said that doing bad stuff during the war didn't feel bad then, at least compared to what was going on otherwise. He was a bit disgusted that now he didn't make enough money to put furniture in all but one room of his giant house, and he just wanted to forget about the war. I quickly gave up on the notion that I was on the brink of shutting down some massive criminal enterprise, and I just started asking about the woodworking. He explained that his uncle was the craftsman responsible for the exquisite woodwork in the house.

The encounter with the Spider, then this man started out as a high intensity cops and robbers kind of ordeal, but as it became more and more personal and we became more and more informed, the whole thing just turned into a sequence of meeting great people with troubled pasts and great personalities.

Of course, the yankee woodworker in me had to meet a fellow wood working craftsman, so I visited him soon thereafter. Over time the woodworker turned out to be a real friend, and connected me with many other great people in the area, Croat and Serb. We got hammered on rakiya and Jack Daniels routinely, and one time the man went back to work at the wood shop drunk after one of our conversations, and severely damaged his hand in a joiner machine. I played with his kids and his huge sarplaninac dogs, and he introduced me to spindle shaper machines. In fact, he offered to give me one of the puppies to take back to America. Deep personal conversations with this man over dinner and drinks led me to another man who used to be great friends with the woodworker prior to the war. Of course, my curiosity sent me to link up with this man as well.

The man was the mayor of a small Serb town called Ignic Mahala, which was a quaint little village on the Republic of Serbia's border to the Orašje Croat pocket. He lived in a small house with his wife and young son, and he did some lightweight farming for sustenance. He was probably 40 or 50 years old, white hair, short and stocky. He was a very soft spoken man who was overtly sad over how the war had changed his country. Every time I went there, which was at least once a week, I was greeted in a way that one treats a friend when they show up at your house. We always drank rakija, and also had bread most times on a small table in his front yard, which provided bucolic pastoral views of the area around his house and the village.

Much of the "front line" fighting between Croat and Serb forces, as well as skirmishes with Muslim forces out of nearby

Gradacac, had occurred in and around my friend's house continuously for several years during the war. There were still bullet holes in certain places in his house and his small barn. I'm disappointed in myself that I cannot remember his name, but I remember he was very patriotic about Bosnia, and was so tired of the war he loved to tell me about Yugoslavia before the war started. He liked to talk about how the Yugoslavian people now have two identities to contend with in their hearts and minds; prewar unified, versus postwar divided.

*My Serb woodworking friend and his family, along with Goran, my Serb interpreter on the left. Photo is mine*

I connected him to one of our Civil Affairs units, and they helped him put a new playground in the village. Of course I asked about the Orašje Mayor and the ostrich farmer, the spider, and the woodworker, and of course he knew them all, and like he always said, before the war there was no problem between anyone. This man introduced me to another important person on my trip, a Sergeant in the Army of the Republic of Serbia (VRS). The VRS had a bad rap, mainly because of the Srebrenica massacre, corrupt leadership, and the media bias against the Bosnian Serbs in general.

The first time I drove into the Bosnian Serb Army compound I was a bit nervous, because these were military Serbs, undoubtedly with ties to people in Serbia, and I assumed intuitively that they would be obligated to be pissed off about the US bombing of Serbia. The compound driveway was comprised of crushed stone mixed with mud. A volleyball net was on the right as I pulled in from the main road, and some low buildings sprawled perpendicular to the street a few hundred yards. As we parked the car, the soldiers, wearing their camouflage pants with only t-shirts, stopped what they were doing to watch us get out of the car. I was a bit nervous, but got out and walked towards a building that looked intuitively like the place one should check into upon arrival. We walked in the door, and a short plump cross-eyed man with very few teeth, exceptionally dirty, stood up somewhat alarmed. There was another man, about 30 or so, dressed in a Serb Army uniform, and he also stood up with an alarmed but under control look on his face.

Using my standard JCO swagger, I smiled and extended my hand, which immediately put them at ease. The man in uniform, a Sergeant, asked if we were there to inspect them, and he was nervous because they were not prepared for an inspection. I laughed at this notion, because this was the first I had learned that the US conventional forces did monthly inspections of the Serb units. I assured him that I wouldn't even consider inspecting them, because in my unit we'd pretty much abandoned the whole concept of inspections. He smiled, and the usual rapport building ensued.

Within minutes we were drinking rakija and talking about what a terrible thing the bombing of Serbia was, and found common ground about what life as a soldier is like. From that point on, we were showing up routinely to play volleyball with the troops, and we bought a few volleyballs in Croatia and gave them to the unit.

The sergeant and I grew into friends. I used to go to his house for dinner at night with Goran and play with his kids and teach them English. I would often bring him Jack Daniels to mix with the rakija. We became so trusting of each other that when we were transitioning out of the country and I brought the new team to meet him, he told them that once I leave he did not want to see any more Americans. He gave me one of his Serb Army uniforms, and told me I was an honorary Serb soldier in his opinion.

One Green Beret

*Bosnian Serb Army Uniform. Given to me by a friend. Photo is from my own collection, taken in my basement.*

I continued to meet people, which led to meeting more people, until within a month or two I was meeting two to three groups of people per day as a general routine. I got drunk on rakija in the morning with someone, sobered up or continued over lunch, then got drunk again in the early afternoon with someone else, and often yet again over dinner and at night. It was not uncommon for me to have a buzz all day. This went on for several months, and I developed an unbelievable tolerance for alcohol. I could easily drink most Serbs and Croats under the table on their own rakija, which I think may border on superhuman.

Things were going great, I must say I kind of fell in love with Serb culture, we were massively successful JCOs, and I actually felt like a legitimate member of the communities that I frequented. Everything was perfect until the Russian Military, who were based in Eastern Bosnia not far from us, suddenly drove from Bosnia into Serbia, causing quite an international ruckus, and prompting my team, and other SF teams, to change missions dramatically. "Operation Vodka Chaser" (OVC) was initiated.

OVC was not just a funny and interesting name. During this little known Special Forces operation, I think we came close to starting World War III. It would have been the second of such a war to begin in the Balkans. Since the Russians were suddenly moving all their troops into Serbia, OVC was basically a "recon mission," to account for the places the Russians were crossing, and to report how many were crossing at each point. I felt like I had been transported back in time to 1991 to boot camp where they were still teaching us that Russia was our greatest enemy.

At first I became very excited, because I thought OVC might be my big chance at war. Our first mission under OVC was to watch the Russians on the Bosnian side of the Drina River near a bridge that crossed into Serbia. Initially, I envisioned myself with camouflage face paint on, perhaps a bayonet in my teeth, crawling through the misty forest or mud to secretly watch the Russian enemy. I was soon disappointed that once we got close enough to see the Russian vehicles lined up for miles on the road it appeared that our only option was to park a "safe" distance away, in plain sight. Soon we got hungry and went to get pizza.

## One Green Beret

One of the guys on my team, a moron obviously in hindsight, pointed his weapon at the Russians in order to use the rifle scope to get a better look: binoculars would have been a less threatening and more intelligent approach, but nevertheless, it happened. Instantly, the Russian troops began to scramble before us, some took cover, and some aimed their rifles back at us. I braced myself for the impact of a bullet, but tried to remain in a non-threatening posture as I looked back at their white round faces under their helmets; they looked so young. If one of them had felt threatened and fired a shot, it would have been a major international incident. Imagine a Russian soldier shooting an American soldier in Bosnia in 1999 as Russia was rolling into Serbia against NATO's wishes. It could have been spun that the Russians had begun to directly support the Serbs against NATO, and the rest would have been history. Since we were just standing there in the street near the car, we scolded the guy for using his weapon in a threatening way because not only was it stupid, but also because there were probably two thousand Russian troops lined up in front of us that would have wiped us out almost instantly. I waved at the mass of Russian troops as if to say "sorry for the confusion guys... don't mind us!" If one of those soldiers had fired a shot, it would have been a significant historical event.

The first night I watched the Russians at the bridge, it was exceptionally dark and rainy, and one of the Russians came to talk to us. He had a blond crew cut, and was average size, with his AK slung over his shoulder. At first I was fearful, since I had been taught for so many years in the Army that Russia was our enemy, until he casually asked for a cigarette in decent English. One of the guys on my team gave him one and the Russian asked what we were doing watching them. I didn't know what to say, so I just told him the truth. My team always seemed to look at me to do the talking in situations like this for some reason. I told the Russian that we were there to count them and let our bosses know when they moved. I described it in a matter of fact kind of way that made it sound like it was just a common military thing we were doing. I figured he would relate to it if I described it like a soldier, because that's what we both were. He laughed, told us how many people were in his unit, and that none of them had a clue when they were crossing, nor where they were going inside Serbia after they did. He said wherever they go, it would sure beat going back to Chechnya and getting his head cut off by Chechen rebels. In essence, they were just doing what they were told, waiting for orders. We ended up having an interesting conversation about how much the Russian soldiers feared being captured by the Chechens.

After a while, we had a few Russian troops around talking about random stuff, and then after a few days more everyone had pretty much abandoned the idea of either of us being a threat to each other, especially since we had so much in common. Dozens of Russians came for cigarettes so we started bringing more with us to hand out on our shifts, and we also brought them a few pizzas. When the Russians began to move into Serbia, a few of them even came over to say goodbye and thank us for the cigarettes. I was confounded by the unstoppable niceness of people if you just talk to them, seemingly regardless of any situation or historical backdrop (i.e, the Cold War). I was starting to think, in a subconscious and unstructured way, that you just can't stop humanity from happening in situations where it's unavoidable to get personal with people.

After the Russians said their goodbyes, and their convoys rattled off across the foggy bridge into Serbia and ultimately Kosovo, with abstract human shapes waving to us in the distance

## One Green Beret

under fuzzy yellow street lights, our mission there in Bosnia was over. I went back to Brčko and sadly fared well to all of my friends and all the people I'd met. I am a serious loner of a guy, and rarely do I let acquaintances turn into real friends, but I did leave some real friends behind in Bosnia. Goran my interpreter, the Serb Sergeant, the Ostrich farmer, the SRS president, the woodworker, and the mayors of Ignic Mahala and Orašje will all be in my memories forever. I will also never forget the priest outside Brčko with the super yellow gas-tasting rakija, how the conventional troops misperceived the riots and everything else about the Serbs, giving our cook's son an IV because he was dehydrated due to drinking nothing but rakiya for over 4 days, the king karajorgiva schnitzel in Šamac, the dead body that floated up to the shore at a restaurant in Orašje, the day we took the chicken-wire and sandbags down from our windows in our house, the party we had with all of our acquaintances across all ethnicities and how much fun they had complaining about the absurdity of the war while they were drunk, the way Goran played my guitar, when Goran brought us to his house to see his room, the destroyed village where Goran was wounded, the amount of trash in the Muslim town of Gradacac and that we actually weren't very welcome there so I didn't go there very often, the stupidity of rebuilding houses when there were no jobs so people would strip the houses to sell the materials for money, how NATO wanted to crush corruption but didn't realize corruption was the only form of post war economy, showing the woodworker how to make a table leg tapering jig the New England way, trying to figure out the human smuggling operations in the area, the old guy who mowed our lawn with a scythe, the old woman cook we hired who we paid better than the Brčko mayor that used to bring us to the market to carry stuff for her, when the SEALs went on a super secret "direct action" mission to blow up a train track and we wondered why we didn't just drive up to the train track and dismantle it while we had a picnic with some of our friends, and the list goes on.

As I was driving towards Sarajevo to leave Bosnia for the second time, staring out the window as people waved from in front of their simple orange or red cupped tile roofed homes, my mind raced as I thought about all the people I got to know so well. I actually became quite sentimental wondering what would happen to them all and if I'd ever see them again. Every day of my life has triggered thoughts that bring me back to my days in Bosnia, watching these brave and very normal people try to recover from a horrid set of circumstances that overcame them like an unstoppable wave, a wave that none of them could ever explain.

With all the political tension we have now in the USA, I worry that something could escalate here just as fast and surprisingly as it did in Bosnia if the politicians and media keep doing what they're doing.

Towards the end of this trip, my wife had completed her Master's degree, and she was changing jobs to be a Spanish teacher at a regular public high school. While I was away, my wife always kept improving herself. She was a newly arrived first generation immigrant from the Dominican Republic, and couldn't speak any English when she arrived, and now she had earned her Master's degree. I felt proud that she was my wife, having succeeded so amazingly in the face of so much difficulty. My wife endured a lot while I was on these trips, she had to take care of everything while I was gone. It would get worse for her too, since she worried about me when I was deployed to these faraway places.

My team didn't have much time between Brčko and getting prepared for our next deployment to Kosovo, but we spent it doing some interesting combat training. I also went to Special Ops Sniper School, and scuba school. I passed pre scuba, but failed the actual "Combat Divers Course" in Key West after literally drowning in the pool during the "one man competence test." I woke up in an ambulance puking up water, and a medic was testing to see if I had feeling in my legs.

We conducted Winter Warfare and Winter Emersion training out in the Rockies, near a place called Taylor Park. Over 20 people in my company were medically evacuated for extreme cold weather injuries when the temperature plummeted to sixty below zero one night. That was the coldest night of my life; it was scary cold, so cold I was afraid to go to sleep because I thought I might never wake up. I also went to Greece for two months to train with the Greek Special Forces, where I learned a lot about the century long hatred that the Greeks and Turks share for each other, as well as how much the Greeks and Serbs have in common regarding Albanians. I couldn't help but wonder what would happen if the normal people from Greece and Turkey could just hang out and talk to each other more. I also got another perspective on the Kosovo situation that was very aligned with Serb thinking – in their opinion we had bombed the wrong side.

Before long, as expected, we were given orders to go to Kosovo, so we began preparations and "pre mission training." My team was given the mission with the most potential for seeing combat; we were assigned The *Russian Liaison Mission*. The mission was interesting because we were going to live in a small house next to, and work jointly with, the Russian military brigade

One Green Beret

in Kosovo Kamenica, perhaps the same Russian unit we watched cross into Serbia during Operation Vodka Chaser.

## Chapter 3
### Kamenica, Kosovo, 2001
### Russian Liaison Team

Kosovo is a small southern province of Serbia that holds a lot of cultural and historical significance to the Serbs. A shallow review of the situation leads a lot of people to think that Kosovo was a different country that the Serbs invaded, when in reality Kosovo is a Serbian province that they acquired circa WW1. Kosovo borders Albania, and throughout many years, Albanians have become the dominant ethnicity rather than Serbs in Kosovo.

The Kosovo Liberation Army (UCK) was a group of Albanian insurgents that fought for independence within Kosovo, with the goal of becoming an independent ethnic Albanian country. They conducted raids, bombings, and terrorist style attacks against Serb authorities, police, and military posts. Essentially, from a Serbian perspective, and a military perspective, the war in Kosovo was actually a straightforward counter-insurgency, or counter-terrorism initiative. The Serbs were trying to defeat the Albanian rebels, and from a more Albanian perspective, the Albanians were trying to fight for freedom inside Serbia. There was also an ethno-religious angle (but mostly ethnic/territorial, not so much religious).

Both sides - at least those you'd call "hardliners" - had the concept of a "Greater Albania" or a "Greater Serbia." These "greaters" were large overlapping geographic areas within the former Yugoslavia and parts of northern Greece that each side believed they were entitled to because of history. This is a common theme in the many parts of the Balkans. Also, in terms of religious differences, Serbs are Orthodox Christian and most Albanians practice Islam (some Albanians are not Muslim, but most in Kosovo are). So due to hundreds year old ethnic, religious, and territorial disputes, there was plenty of manmade hate to go around, and of course, each side's politicians, Serb and Albanian, leveraged these factors and the media to further the divide. The Serbs argued that the Albanians were terrorists trying to take over the most important province of their country, and the Albanians in Kosovo claimed that the Serbs were oppressing them because of their religion and ethnicity.

Once the Kosovo war started from within Serbia, the Serbian tactics (to be more precise, the way those tactics were *described on the news*), were adequate to once again generate a claim for genocide. There were also many other interesting US politics going on at the time, the one most notable was the Monica Lewinsky scandal. This incident led to the conspiracy theory that the only reason we attacked Serbia was to take attention off the Lewinsky scandal. Another theory is that the claim of genocide was just a tool to legitimize action against someone, anyone, in the world, to look like a moral authority and to maintain positive perception of NATO's legitimacy. Of course, since stopping genocide aligns easily to the concepts of "just war" theory, it wasn't long before NATO was bombing Serbia into the Stone Age for defending their own country, without the backing of the UN Security Council. The bombings actually occurred back in 1999 when I was in Brčko, Bosnia, as per the last chapter.

As for the team dynamic, it is important to know that in the time between Bosnia and Kosovo, my team became incredibly tight, and our Green Beret warrior spirit had been completely refreshed and bolstered by the year worth of brutal training and other experiences we endured together. Being a member of the Green Berets was very similar to being a professional athlete, except that instead of dreaming about the big *game*, I dreamt about the big *war*, like "Olympians with guns" in body, and spirit. One of the reasons my team was assigned the Russian LCE mission was because of our reputation as being "bad-asses" to the extreme. Since the Russian LCE mission had a high probability for achieving a war like state of affairs, my team was the logical choice for the task. In Special Forces, each team develops sort of its own culture and personality, and leadership knowns which teams naturally fit which types of missions.

So with this as the background, we flew into Macedonia via Germany, and made our way into Kosovo to become part of KFOR; it was March of 2001 when we arrived. In a similar fashion to how we traveled to Bihać and Brčko, we took SUVs along the road from Skopje all the way north past Gilanje, and north into Kamenica.

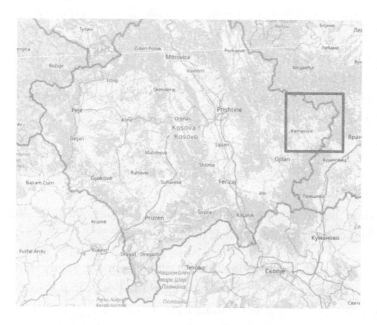

*My team's sector, and the Russian Military sector, approximately (Map source: OpenStreetMap)*

As we drove north from Macedonia, I noticed that Bosnia was much more advanced and generally cleaner than Kosovo. Kosovo looked like you'd imagine a third world country would look like. There were destroyed buildings everywhere like in Bosnia, but the difference was in the interesting volume of trash everywhere. Signs were randomly in Cyrillic or Albanian, and it seemed like the areas with Cyrillic signs (Serb areas) were much cleaner and generally more organized. There was an American base called Camp Bondsteel, but I only saw it a few times while I was there, and as a rule we always tried to keep our distance from conventional forces.

Kamenica was a small village with one main street, and it was nestled into the mountain backdrop along a decent sized river. The big Russian base was on the right side of the road as one approached from the south. Our house was up the main road from the Russian base, and it was across from another smaller Russian compound. When we first arrived in our SUVs, the other team that we would be replacing met us downstairs. The team we were there to replace had actually gotten into a small firefight with Albanian rebels prior to our arrival, and I was very excited to hear about it.

We eventually settled in, and soon thereafter we met the Russian leadership team. My Captain was very proficient in Russian; he was a graduate of the Defense Language Institute, so he was our interpreter most of the time.

It was strange to me that I would be working jointly with the Russians in Kosovo, after being taught in boot camp back in 1991 that killing Russians should be my primary goal in life. Although interaction with Russian troops during Operation

Vodka Chaser had taught me that they were vastly human like we were.

Our overall mission in Kosovo was simple: constantly patrol the Kosovo/Serbia border of the Russian sector jointly with the Russian Army, but don't go into the DMZ. The DMZ was established by NATO, to put some distance between Serbian forces and Kosovo.

The DMZ, of course, made a perfect safe haven for the successors of the UCK who called themselves the *Liberation Army of Preševo, Medveđa, and Bujanovac* (UCPMB). Preševo, Medveđa, and Bujanovac were simply villages in the Presevo Valley that were within or very near the province of Kosovo or within the DMZ. So our mission was clear to me; this UCPMB group was the cause of unrest, and success was defined by disrupting their operations. We decided for ourselves that the best way to keep the peace was to *remove* the UCPMB. In the Green Berets, we drive our own operations with our own intelligence (and sometimes our own perception of the intelligence).

The operations room was where we kept our guns, ammo, the radio to communicate with our headquarters, maps, documents, and other sensitive information and technologies; nothing out of the ordinary in terms of military implements of war. We pulled shifts in the operations room to maintain 24/7 communications with our headquarters, and to monitor other traffic so we had "situational awareness" about things like helicopter flight schedules, and other operations. Since we were in the Russian's area of responsibility in Kosovo, there wasn't any US activity other than a few random helicopter patrols.

There was a giant water blivet in the back yard of the house that fed our plumbing system, and a good sized tent that held a gym full of workout equipment. There was also a small deck, and from the deck I could see five or six other people's small houses. We were living in a development that was like a 3$^{rd}$ world suburbia of sorts. I frequently waved to our neighbors, all Albanians, as they hung cloths out to dry or played with their kids in the small dirt backyards.

In one of the rooms downstairs there was a secret room that was only accessible by a hidden door in the back of a closet. We made this room into a bar, which we lovingly named "The Big Whiskey." We also had email during this trip so I was able to communicate with my wife fairly easily. We sent each other a lot of email, some in Spanish.

Soon it was time for our very first patrol with the Russians. The Russians showed up in a light track vehicle and jumped out. They were big dudes, with headwraps, and blue and white striped t-shirts. They walked confidently, some had gold teeth, and their weapons and equipment were clean; they were sharp. They were Airborne (VDV) as well as Spetznaz (to this day I do not fully understand the structure of Spetznaz, VDV, and how those concepts overlap). We shook hands and exchanged simple greetings in Russian. We loaded into two Armored Hummers and I stood in the turret behind a MK19 automatic grenade launcher.

The roads along the border were single lane dirt roads at best, in most cases it would be more appropriate to call them trails. The trails were very rough and muddy, so we were four wheeling the whole way, which grew rapidly annoying because I was getting thrashed in the turret. On Kitka's peak we sat and ate lunch with the Russians, drank some vodka, listened to their stories of Chechnya, and admired a great view of the beautiful Serbian landscape. I quickly realized why the Serbs love Kosovo so much and didn't want to give it up – it's beautiful.

In the sprawling rural scene below me I saw quaint red roofed villages and small farms nestled into the hills, pastoral views, and also a Serb checkpoint or two. On this first day I manned the turret for over 10 hours, bouncing along the border to the DMZ. I saw absolutely nothing but beautiful countryside and friendly people herding goats on small farms.

After the prior team left Kosovo, my team started to build rapport significantly with the Russian Spetznaz soldiers and the Russian officer leadership. The old team was not able to build the same kind of relationship we did because they didn't have my Captain's unique ability to fully communicate with them in their native language. The Spetznaz and VDV were the Russian equivalent to the Green Berets or SEALs (I think), and there was some natural synergy because of this, and a bit of competition. I believe we all barely survived one such incident of competition without being seriously injured.

The Russians had a special thing they called a banya. A banya is basically a sauna on steroids (perhaps *literally* in this case) in which it is not uncommon that the small steam room becomes hot enough to actually cause serious injury – scary hot. So, guess what happens when the Russian Spetznaz invite the US Army Green Berets over to the banya? Well, you get a bunch of large naked and stinky men in a steam room wearing fuzzy Russian hats and drinking vodka, the intensity of the heat progresses to downright dangerous as vodka consumption increases, and you wait to see who the last person standing is before someone literally dies or becomes seriously injured.

Not only did we brave the perils of the steam room until near death, but periodically they made us run, totally naked, outside and jump into a giant tank of cold water, just to prove we were too tough for it to give us a heart attack. I am proud to say that my team ultimately won, but I must admit it was not me who outlasted the Russians. I was just happy to survive with my skin still attached, lungs still functioning after breathing the searing hot air, and heart still beating. One interesting thing about these rapport building excursions was the unbelievable amount of commonality we had as human beings. I wondered, why were these people our enemy for so many decades?

One day while drinking peppermint vodka with one of the Russians on our back deck after a long patrol, one of them asked if we had been scared that Russia might actually bomb the US with nuclear ICBMs back in the 80s, and he had a serious look on his face and tone in his voice. I was a little stunned by the bluntness of the question, but I answered honestly that I really didn't think so. The Russian guy chuckled, in a somewhat annoyed way, and proceeded to tell us how imminent they thought a US attack really was. Because, as he explained, we *did* nuke Japan, why wouldn't we nuke Russia?

The magnitude of the rapport we built with the Russians was incredible, we had open conversations like this all the time, in fact there were instances where my Captain found himself in meetings where he claimed that they had forgotten he was an American altogether, and they were exchanging Russian classified information right in front of him. My next story will illustrate this level of trust in another interesting way.

One day, the Russian Colonel came to our house to take my Captain somewhere special. Since we never travel alone, my

Captain brought another member of my team with him. The three of them and an interpreter drove in a small Russian jeep north - further north than any of us had ever been. My teammate that had gone with my Captain said he took a reading on his GPS and the grid coordinate plotted them over 10 Kilometers into Serbia, and he quickly realized that they had gone all the way through the DMZ and out the other side into "Serbia Proper," which we as US troops were strictly forbidden from doing. We knew that the Serbs and the Russians had a history of strong ties, so apparently the Russian colonel felt comfortable just driving into Serbia as if it was normal. The problem was, we were still basically at war with Serbia (or at least that's what we thought *the Serbs* would think), so my teammates grew increasingly concerned as the vehicle continued relentlessly north through the hills of southern Serbia.

After driving for quite some time, In the distance, they saw what looked like a large military checkpoint, and as they grew closer, it became apparent that it was a sizable Serbian Army outpost. My Captain thought they were about to be handed over to the Serbs as prisoners. They pulled up to the Serb checkpoint and stopped, and the Russian colonel got out of the vehicle.

The Russian Colonel and a Serbian commander spoke for a while as numerous Serbian soldiers curiously gathered and peered into the jeep. My captain readied a frag grenade, and he and my teammate quickly planned how they would throw grenades and try to run south as fast as they could if bad things happened; likely dying or being captured in the process. What happened next is a miracle of sorts. Apparently, the Russian Colonel had described to the Serbian officer our absolute commitment to ridding Kosovo of the Albanian rebels and what great work we had done so far, and the Serbs seemed to like that. The Serbs said that as long as they weren't the pilots who destroyed their country, my two teammates were ok to continue to live. Then the Serbs broke out some classic Rakiya to take the edge off.

Right there on the side of that dirt road in Serbia, where US troops weren't supposed to be due to imminent danger and international agreements, a Russian Spetznaz colonel, a couple US Green Berets, and some Serbian Soldiers (all sworn enemies at some point in recent history) sipped rakija while they talked about how insane the cold war was, how absurd the bombings of Serbia were, how much they hate politicians, and how amazing it was that they were all allies during World War two. They got a little tipsy, and had to back off on the rakija before exchanging "I love you guys" man-hugs with the Serbs, and making the drive back into Kosovo. The meeting was also productive, because as they gulped rakija they also exchanged information about where the UCPMB was operating. *Oh, the humanity.*

Apparently, word spread fast among the Serbs about this meeting in the hinterlands of Serbia, because from that point on we had Serb checkpoints in the distance waving at us as we drove the border. Also, some of our other teams had reported that the UCPMB morale was low because now they thought that the Russians, US Special Forces, and Serbs had joined forces against them. This fueled our resolve to continue our hunting operations along the border, and we just kept hoping for the big game... which would come soon enough.

One day one of the Russian spetznaz burst into our house and told us that they needed our help to evacuate a dead Russian soldier who had been shot by a UCPMB sniper while on patrol. We didn't ask any questions and we set out to get to the area where we could call in a medevac. I was in the Gym working out and listening to death metal when my Team Sergeant rushed in and said something picturesque like "I really need you on this one G-man." I got serious, put on my gear, and took to the turret, and our vehicle soon joined with a large convoy of Russian tracks, trucks, and jeeps headed for the scene of the incident.

We struggled through brutal roads and mud, and arrived an hour or two later, on the top of a grassy ridge overlooking rolling hills, and then we searched for a proper Helicopter Landing Zone (HLZ) nearby. We identified a sufficient HLZ that was a good distance away from the scene, then we called for a chopper to evacuate the Russian soldier. The Russians were all very emotional and yelling things to each other that I couldn't understand.

As I rode the turret to the HLZ, many vehicles got stuck in the mud several times, and we had to continuously get them out for what seemed like hours on end. Finally, we got to the HLZ, and the helicopter flew in and landed very dramatically. This was when I saw, for the first time in my life, a combat-related fatality.

The dead Russian had been shot in the upper face and the exit wound was on the back of his head; I could tell because I saw a hair covered skull fragment swinging by the skin under his head. Four of his comrades pulled him out of a truck and carried him face up, each holding an arm or leg, across the several hundred feet of grass to the chopper. His lifeless body jiggled unnaturally as blood, and fragments of grey brain matter fell out of the back of his head. His eyes didn't move at all, and his body was unresponsive to their touch. The dark fluid left a sparse trail on the grassy ground behind them as they ran for the chopper. As they got closer the rotors of the aircraft blew several Russian's hats off, and the grass around their feet swayed impetuously under the force of wind. Their hunched forms deposited their friend's body into the loud chopper, and then they ran back towards my location, not caring about their lost hats.

My reaction to the scene came mostly in the form of anger, or at least that was the only emotion I was capable of defining for myself at the time. The anger and the scene before me created or reinforced the notions that the UCPMB Albanians were the enemy; an enemy that was worthy of being feared. All those stories the Serbs in Bosnia told me about Albanians in Kosovo made sense at that moment.

After the US helicopter took off with the Russian soldier's body, the four young Russian troops walked past our vehicle, some of them in tears, and soon thereafter we left in a large convoy for a very quiet trip back to Kamenica. Once we got back to the house, we had a very somber meeting, and we all reminded each other that this wasn't a game.

In the next few days, while on a routine patrol, we revisited the spot where the Russian had been sniped, and one of the Russians pointed out where he thought the shot had come from. The location was about 800 yards north of the road; which meant the sniper had made one hell of a long shot. The skill it would have taken to make a shot like that, especially with the typical rifle a UCPMB guy would use, made me curious.

A few days later, on the way back from a typical excursion around the border, I was riding in the turret as usual, and we encountered an Albanian man, about 25 years old, who was exceptionally dirty, and wearing a green military belt walking in the middle of nowhere down a dirt road. The Russians decided to question the man and search his car, and they found evidence that he was a UCPMB member.

The Russians took him into their vehicle, and then they drove him, with our vehicle following behind, back to the Russian base near our house. This was all very intense. Within an hour, the man told the Russians and my Captain the exact location of a UCPMB base camp, and he said that anywhere between 40 and 80 fighters were operating out of it. My adrenaline surged when my Captain said it was "go time." We rushed back to our house and loaded all the ammo we could carry in our hummers. I jumped into the turret behind a MK19 automatic grenade launcher, and we set out to disrupt the base camp as fast as the roads would allow. In unconventional warfare one of the basic principles is speed, if you don't act immediately, the situation will change because the enemy is always adapting and moving. Generally, this is why conventional forces are largely ineffective against unconventional threats. We were headed to a small area in northern Kosovo called Velja Glava.

As we approached the area where the base camp was supposed to be, I saw nothing out of the ordinary. In fact, I had driven by the spot dozens of times. However, one of the Russians noticed a faint indication of tire tracks that ran north through the grassy open area over a hill towards a thick forest. Every map we had in our possession depicted a slightly different line that defined the boundary of Kosovo, but we quickly decided we could go a few hundred meters along the subtle tracks and still be "in bounds," so we followed the tracks uphill towards a barely perceivable opening in the dense evergreens.

As the rumbling Humvee came over the crest of the hill, with me in the turret, my heart surged so hard I thought it might rupture. Those faint tire tracks turned into a very narrow but worn tunnel-like trail leading into the thick evergreen forest, and there was a makeshift wooden gate blocking the way. The rickety gate had a square sign nailed to it with the words "STOP, UCPMB!" crudely painted onto it in bright red. My eyes immediately shifted to a very young man who was guarding the gate; he wore a colorful camouflage uniform and a red beret with a UCPMB patch on it, and he carried an AK. He stared up at me with his eyes as big as oranges and mouth agape in disbelief.

Before I could move, two of my teammates jumped out of our vehicle. One ripped the sign off the fence and smashed the gate out of the way, while the other simultaneously apprehended and disarmed the young UCPMB guy. The Spetznaz, who were right behind me on top of a Russian vehicle called a BTR, rapidly dismounted, and with the chatter of frantic Russian, they ran into the woods to my left. A commotion ensued in the trees in front of us, and I saw indications and impressions of movement everywhere before me. Everyone in both of our Humvees dismounted except for the drivers and the gunners. I was gunner on the lead vehicle, the driver lurched forward, then we started creeping forward towards the center of what I quickly realized was a base camp that probably covered 5 or 6 acres of thick forest. This was no joke.

My heart quaked as I listened to dozens of Albanians shouting feverishly everywhere from the forest in front of me, but I couldn't see any of them. My senses were pegged, and my eyes moved frantically in response to every micro sound I heard. I noticed a small car that was cleverly camouflaged into the trees, and several tents, all under small botanical bubbles that were carved very cunningly into the extremely dense canopies of the very large evergreen trees. The purr of the hummer's engine and the sound of my own pulse made it hard to hear anything clearly. My Captain asked our interpreter what they were all saying, and he said he really couldn't tell. The interpreter said he thought some of them were speaking Persian Farsi so he couldn't understand. At the time, I had no idea where people that spoke Persian came from, and I was too busy scanning the woods in front of me to think about it.

Suddenly, to my front I heard the popping of gun fire and the subsequent sound of bullets streaming through the trees; the whizzing and snapping sound blended with the sound of the purr of the hummer beneath me. It sounded like the bullets were streaming past me, but because of the Hummer engine, and since I had never heard the sounds of bullets flying past me before, I wasn't completely sure. Within a fraction of a second, a few more rounds whizzed by, and I became convinced they *were* shooting at us. My whole body tensed, and I clenched my teeth so hard I felt the roots poke up into my jaw. I braced my body in anticipation, as the fear of being shot swept over me.

I ducked down low in the turret and swung the MK19 cannon towards the general direction of the fire, towards the thick evergreens in front of me, and towards a bend in the path about 75 meters ahead. I was scared to death, and a vision of the dead Russian soldier's lifeless body and dripping head wound flashed into my mind. I thought of my wife, my team's safety, and I imagined bullets ripping through my flesh. Suddenly the overwhelming perception that I *had to act now* took over my senses.

I became furious, more furious than I thought was humanly possible, and I made the decision to return suppressive fire, based on what I felt and what I thought I knew about the situation. The unprecedented combination of fear and rage further brimmed as I flipped the safety off and started to depress those cool steel butterfly triggers on the MK19 machine gun. I was wearing my fingerless black leather gloves, and the steel butterfly triggers felt cool on the tips of my thumbs.

In slow motion, I felt the weight of the weapon's bolt slide forward once I depressed the triggers far enough to cause its release. I heard the cannon roar and watched it belch fire. I felt the bolt rhythmically rock back and forth as it pulled round after belted round into the chamber and hurled them unmercifully towards the trees. The forest in front of me lit up with incredibly loud and concussive explosions of fire and smoke from the barrage of 40 millimeter grenade rounds that flew from my weapon as I cussed in fury at the hidden enemy before me. A few other guys on my team returned fire as well. I reloaded the weapon robotically, subconsciously, and continued to fire. In less than a minute all the firing stopped when my Captain called cease fire. My heart rate was alarmingly high, my ears rang at a feverish pitch, and my adrenaline was so pegged I was tingling all over and felt weightless. The forest in front of me was smoking and branches were still falling off trees even after the firing had stopped.

My team sergeant, Frank, started yelling orders to secure the perimeter of the camp, and my captain was speaking Russian into a radio. I dismounted and grabbed the M240 machine gun from inside the Hummer as I rushed to exit the vehicle. I ran north about 75 yards through the botanical tunnels that connected the multitude of interwoven bed-down sites within the base camp. I reached the end of the green kaleidoscopic tunnel and stopped at what appeared to be the edge of the base camp. I noticed there were old bloody bandages on the ground, and I assumed they were from wounded UCPMB fighters that had recently returned from attacks on Serb checkpoints nearby. The rest of my team and the Russians were conducting a detailed search of the camp, and for the next few minutes I just kneeled next to a big evergreen tree, and faced outward waiting for a counter attack. I thought through every scenario I could imagine... a sniper taking me out, perhaps watching me every moment in his crosshairs, getting captured and taken off to some evil place, and I even thought the whole area may be rigged with explosives and we may all explode at any second. I had never been so tense in my life.

Within a minute my team called me back to the hummers, and I helped pull a mortar tube out of the ground. Then I saw something harrowing.

The Russians had captured several UCPMB members, and they were marching them past us towards their vehicle. I saw that several of the men were injured, with lots of blood on their faces and one had an injured hand. One had blood running out of his hand onto the ground. The blood was darker than I thought it would be. I realized that maybe it had been *me* that injured these people – things got real. As they walked by me one of the Albanian men looked into my eyes and we connected to each other's stare. His face was heavy with doom and fear and blood, and his eyes pleaded to me. In that tiny instant when our eyes met, it was like he silently begged me to explain to him what the hell just happened, and why. I looked away and continued to drive through the situation.

We weren't there more than 20 more minutes, and we loaded the vehicles and backed out of the base camp the same way we entered. A guy on my team who had lost his grenade the day we medevac-ed the dead Russian soldier found it in one of the tents inside the center of the base camp. This tent was full of an amazing amount and variety of large munitions like landmines and mortar shells. This could have caused a massive explosion, and we were very lucky that one of my grenades did not hit this tent.

We captured 8 or 9 of the UCPMB members that day at Velja Glava. Several of them were injured by shrapnel or bullet wounds. We drove them back to the Russian base, and I went back to our house still completely pumped with adrenaline. The Russian Spetznaz team immediately came over and said that my fire was perfect for covering their advances on the left flank. When they said this I was alarmed, because it was pure luck that my fire was helpful to them. I had no idea where they had gone once they entered the forest (although my Captain likely did). In fact, I think we were all surprised that I didn't hit any of them by mistake.

This was the first firefight that I experienced as a Green Beret and as a soldier. At the time it was a very big deal to have seen "combat," because this took place prior to 911 and very few Green Berets could say they'd ever seen combat. The Russians further interrogated each of the captives, and we conducted several more follow-on operations in the next few days based on tips from the captured, none of which amounted to much in comparison to what happened at Velja Glava.

The Big Whiskey's character completely changed after that day. In our minds we had all become real warriors. We built a table out of a captured machine (DsHK) gun tripod. We hung uniforms of the UCPMB on the wall for display. We hung a reconstructed belt of some of my MK19 round casings proudly on the back wall. Frank had captured the ultimate prize, the "STOP UCPMB!" sign, and we hung it in the Big Whiskey as well. We even decided that now the Russians were worthy of coming into the Big Whiskey, and we frequently invited them to drink beer and listen to Johnny Cash as we uncovered the infinite layers of detail concerning the Velja Glava incident. Afterwards, I thought that the intense dreams I had just came with the territory of being a real warrior.

A few weeks later, the UCPMB gave up and turned in their weapons. Moreover, NATO decided to close down the DMZ as part of a deal with the Serbs and an attempt to keep the Albanians in control, because they were again causing trouble in Macedonia as well. I basked in the notion that it was our single act of brutally decisive violence at Velja Glava that made them realize that they could not withstand the pressures of the Russians, the US Special Forces, and the Serbs all at once. Our egos were quite inflamed.

A few weeks later, we were part of the operation of linking up with Serbian forces as part of NATO eliminating the DMZ. When we went on this operation, for some reason the conventional Army guys accompanied us. As the three or four Serbs that were sent to link up with us approached on foot on the dirt road, the conventional troops trained all their weapons on them. We adamantly yelled at the young troops who were aiming at the alarmed Serbs in order to make them stop. I find it interesting now, that the conventional troops held the belief that the Serbs were the enemy, while at the same time we held the complete opposite belief. This was a good example of how significant the divide between conventional and SOF units can be.

The Serbs were very excited to meet Americans, and I shook all their hands as we exchanged pleasantries and smiles in Serbian. They were surprised and impressed at how well I could speak some basic Serbian phrases (due to spending over a year in Bosnia). They had very clean weapons and equipment, and seemed very professional. They told us and the Russians all the locations they would patrol, and we exchanged other types of military information such as potential UCPMB locations. They had a natural rapport with the Russians. This was all very ironic.

Since the Serbs had arrived on foot, I offered to give them a ride back to their checkpoint in our Hummer, an idea that the conventional guys thought was insane. Regardless, the Serbs and I all piled into our hummer and we drove a few miles to their checkpoint and we dropped them off. As the Serbian troops walked away I flashed the three finger hand symbol to them, this made one of the Serb soldiers openly excited and he high fived one of his buddies. The three finger hand symbol is when you hold out only your thumb, index, and middle fingers, palm facing outward, thus making a V with the index and middle finger, and a J with the shape of the index and thumb together; it was something I had learned in Bosnia from my Serbian sergeant friend. This is a very important part of Serbian culture, founded in the holy trinity, but now has a more general purpose of expressing, ultimately, pride in being Serbian.

Towards the end of our tour in Kosovo, some interesting conversations occurred between my Captain and the Russians that he frequently spoke to. The conversation led me to believe that the death of the Russian soldier by the Albanian sniper may have been a hoax. In fact, it was suspected that another Russian soldier may have murdered the soldier I had seen carried to the helicopter, or it was a suicide, or accidental discharge. One thing that had been suspicious to me was the precision of the shot; it would have taken a very skilled marksman with a high-end rifle to make a shot like that (without luck). I am/was a trained special forces sniper (Special Operations Target Interdiction Course (SOTIC) graduate), and to imagine a UCPMB guy with a clunky soviet SVD rifle making a shot like that seemed unlikely (although possible). I was alarmed at this new info, because the fact that a Russian had been killed by "the enemy" had really legitimized all the operations we'd been doing against the UCPMB as well as my entire mentality. If I had known about this prior to Velja Glava, would I have pulled the trigger?

It would be absurd to imagine the Albanian resistance ever quitting. The UCPMB merely turned in a fraction of their weapons to make it appear that they had quit, and so they could go into a latent and insipient state until NATO departed. It made sense; NATO was on the verge of taking Kosovo from Serbia and giving it to them, why would they want to piss us off?

As I reflect on Kosovo now, I feel some guilt for the injuries I may have caused on Velja Glava. Sometimes I think maybe if we had just taken the JCO approach and smiled at that young guy at the gate, and asked if we could talk to whomever was in charge, then we'd probably have found ourselves drinking tea in the middle of that base camp, and things probably would have ended up about the same as they did except no one would have gotten hurt. However, at the same time I can't help but remember that, then, I truly felt like my team and I were in grave danger that day on Velja Glava. They were shooting at us, and I had absolutely no doubt I needed to return fire to protect my team and preserve my own life. Also, just maybe the decision the UCPMB made to go back into remission would not have happened if we hadn't done what we did that day, and maybe that was good. Maybe the UCPMB going into remission was a good thing and maybe it was bad or maybe it was progress.

Today, from a macro level, I don't think that the US should have ever been involved in Kosovo in the first place, and to be totally honest, I personally view what we did to Serbia as very hypocritical. However, it's hard to dismiss the fact that we now have a huge base in one of the most historically strategic locations on earth – the southern Balkans. Maybe that was the point all along.

Soon enough, we were on our way back to Macedonia, and then Colorado. My wife and I moved into a different house as soon as I got home.

# Chapter 4
## 2002, 2003
### From after Kosovo to Iraq

When I returned from Kosovo, feeling proud that other teams were envious that we'd seen some combat, my team changed a bit. Frank left the team and moved to North Carolina, to be an instructor at the Special Forces Intel course (18F) at FT Bragg, and I was promoted to E7 and became the "acting" Team Sergeant. Frank was respected and loved by the whole team and by everyone in the 10$^{th}$ Special Forces Group. He died of throat cancer in 2012 after surviving three tours in Iraq. He was a true leader and an absolute badass. He always looked past my stupidity and listened to what I had to say with genuine interest. I will never forget him.

After a short recovery period and some leave, we started the usual cycle of high intensity training in the Colorado mountains and the shooting ranges on Ft. Carson. I attended a course referred to as Sniper Sustainment Training, which existed so qualified Spec Ops snipers could keep their skills sharp. My team also parachuted into Alaska, went to the Northern Warfare Training Center's mountaineering course, and then fished for King Salmon. We also got a new company commander, who was known for his out of the box thinking, charisma, and open minded approach to leadership.

One of the things I remember most about this new company commander is that he was very friendly to everyone, and always seemed to engage in conversation with people in the same way regardless of their rank. In his eyes, everyone was assumed to be potentially smart until they proved themselves otherwise.

## One Green Beret

The great officers always had a few significant properties: they were genuinely interested in what their subordinates thought, and their interest was genuine because they were smart enough to know that they did not have all the answers. However, although they were humble, they knew that their opinion mattered because they were in charge. They also never catered to anyone just to be nice; they were out to solve the problem in the most logical way possible, regardless of where the ideas came from. Since they valued their own admittedly imperfect ideas, they almost always showed up with *the first idea* and it usually carried a lot of logic and intelligence with it. This company commander was one of these people: a highly humble, passionate, intellectual, and competent professional. I've tried to live up to these qualities in my post military life as a technology leader.

One morning in the Sniper Sustainment course, while preparing to go out to the firing range, the news was on the TV in the room, and we watched a plane fly into one of the twin towers in NYC.

Like everyone else in the country, we thought it was an accident. But then the second plane hit.

Instantly, it became common knowledge that we had been deliberately attacked. Everyone in the room, sniper rifles in hand and ghillie-suit pants on, preparing to go to the range, standing in complete silence, eyes glued to the TV screen, instantly knew that our lives were about to change. We all started debating who would ship out first, our unit or the 5th Special Forces Group. Everyone in the room wanted to be on the next plane to somewhere to kill whoever did this. At first, we thought we should all head back to our team rooms and wait for orders, but instead we just trained as planned. We spent the day at the range, and I felt newfound reason and motivation to improve my skills.

I was disappointed when I found out that my unit (10$^{th}$ Group) was not going to be the first to ship out and go after the people who had attacked us. I was intensely jealous when I saw 5$^{th}$ Special Forces Group teams on the news a few months later riding horseback with the Afghan Northern Alliance and taking on the Taliban. I had never heard of Al Qaida nor the Taliban until 911, and I had never heard of this notion that there were "islamists" out in the world who hated us. Since I had lived with thousands of Bosnian and Albanian Muslims none of it made sense to me. We waited in angst.

Soon, my team got a new Team Sergeant, and we were sent on a Foreign Internal Defense mission to Kyrgyzstan as part of OEF. During this trip we had an issue with the new team sergeant, and we had a big confrontation. This confrontation was borderline mutiny on my part, and because of this when we returned the team was split up, and I was moved to the B-Team. A "B-Team" is the company headquarters team for an SF company, and of course I had no desire to be on the B-Team, because they take care of mostly administrative stuff. I hated being on the B-Team, but it gave me something I hadn't ever had: time.

One day, my wife made a casual suggestion that I should try and get some college work done at night, since I now had more time. The next day I went to the base education center, and I signed up to start an AAS at the Pikes Peak Community College in Colorado Springs. One good thing about being a happy-go-lucky, albeit not so smart, hard-charger, was that I never let anything get to me for very long. Fundamentally, I have always been highly capable of not giving a damn about things I cannot control, and obsessively seizing opportunities when I *did* have control; this was one of those occasions.

Within a few weeks, I found myself in several college classes at different times per week. I took some math, information systems, English composition, and some other basic courses. However, the most memorable class by far that I took was Sociology. I will never forget the first paper I wrote in that class, which, at age 28, was the first college paper I had ever written in my life. The professor, a woman, gave me a C-Minus grade. She basically slaughtered me in every single way possible on her critique and revealed to me with amazing clarity just how intellectually challenged I was. This was one of the defining moments in my life, reading her harsh comments on my paper, then reading my shallow writing that prompted the comments, and reflecting on the two made my heart and mind race, almost like I could smell the paper burning as I read it. Initially I was furious, I felt like I'd been insulted or something. I thought to myself, how dare she! I was a *real Green Beret* damn it! However, the more I read and digested her comments, the more I realized how right she was. I wasn't a person who liked to lose, so her comments propelled me on a mission to prove her wrong. I worked very hard, harder than I had ever worked on anything academic in my life. I ended up getting an A in the class. I had been introduced to the concept of logical thinking and structured analysis, and although I didn't acknowledge it then, *I was actually pretty good at it.* I finished an AAS and fell in love with academics and the power of education.

Around the time I finished my AAS, and as tensions in Iraq were escalating, a very strong Team Sergeant had taken over my old team. Then my old ODA also got assigned a mission to go into Northern Iraq. It was the kind of mission that every Green Beret dreams about. Within a day or two, he managed to convince the Sergeant Major somehow to let me back on the team. Soon enough I was back in business, man-hugs abounded as I moved my kit back into my old team room. I felt a rush of energy from the anticipation; this was the real deal.

Just when I thought I had secured my spot in war, I injured my back and neck so severely on a parachute drop soon after rejoining my old team that I was dragged off the drop zone to the emergency room.

When I hit the ground I was knocked out for second, then I thought I was paralyzed from the neck down because I couldn't move for about a minute. The parachute dragged me across the ground for several hundred feet before it stopped. When I was being dragged by the parachute, feeling numb or tingly from the neck down, I wasn't thinking that I might be paralyzed for life or any of the associated long term consequences of that. Instead, the only thing on my mind was that I might not be able to go to war with my team if this injury was too bad.

The medics rushed out onto the drop zone and put me on a stretcher; I could barely move when they reached me. They drove me to the base hospital's ER where they gave me a checkup as the feeling came back to my body. I had compressed my neck and back and produced three bulged disks in my neck. Although I was in amazing pain, I pretended it didn't hurt and they gave me naproxen. I took a few weeks off from doing PT and sucked it up.

As we began intense planning and training for our special mission in Iraq I got better at ignoring the pain in my neck and back, my wife grew more and more pregnant, and my grandmother more and more sick. My old Captain left on some special operation in Tajikistan so we soon received a new Captain. The new young Captain was very sharp and fit right in, although the strong team sergeant gave him a bit of a hard time sometimes – which is pretty normal is SF.

On September 11$^{th}$ 2002, my wife called the team room and told me her water had broken. It was a miracle that I was in the team room and available to take the call, I did not have a cell phone then. I rushed home, picked her up, along with all of that stuff you're supposed to bring to the hospital when you expect to bring a baby home, and we sped off to the hospital in my Ford truck. Within only a few hours I watched my daughter blast out of my wife, writhing beautifully in blood, and other forms of unidentifiable excrement. She was choking, so the doctors had to remove some material from her throat so she could breathe, which scared me. I counted her fingers and toes, and within a few seconds, I had declared her *perfect*: the word I used to describe her to everyone I told her about from that point forward. We named her Angela Rafaela, because Rafaela was my grandmother's name, and my wife's mother's middle name. Angela was also the name of a sister my wife had in the Dominican Republic that unfortunately died at around the age of 18 months when my wife was a child there.

Suddenly the thought of going to Iraq scared me a little. This was the first time in my life that the real world nudged its way into my quest for war, and I wasn't sure what to make of it.

My daughter was a miracle, but unfortunately (for her) she was extremely colicky. My wife and I took turns staying up all night and trying to calm her down and get her to sleep. I fondly remember sitting in the moonlight rubbing her belly trying to calm her down; the way she looked into my eyes and connected with me was amazing.

As part of my pre mission training for Iraq, I had to go to the hinterlands of Colorado for a two-week rehearsal exercise, and during that trip my wife got very sick. She spent several nights alone in a fever trying to calm down an exceptionally difficult baby, with no way to contact me and no idea where I was. It wouldn't be until much later in life that I realized just how much my wife had to endure because of my lifestyle as a Green Beret.

Soon after my daughter was born, my grandmother died. I was very close to her, and I felt like part of what defined me as a human being had disappeared. When my mother called and told me she had passed, I suddenly felt so sad that it physically hurt me and it literally took my breath away. It bothered me tremendously that she never got to see my daughter because we lived in Colorado. I flew back to Connecticut for the funeral.

We were very close, and I cried at the site of her in the open casket, remembering how we used to play go-fish together, and how she loved my wife and used to call her Ziggy. My father and brother convinced me that if I had seen her during the months leading up to her death, I would have agreed that it was a good thing that she died. They had witnessed her deterioration and that helped them cope, whereas I last remembered her as an active, funny, and loving little 4 foot 10 Italian grandma who thought the world of me even with all my blatant imperfections. I was crushed, but I returned to Colorado, wiped away the tears, and put my war face back on.

Finally, I was given notice of when my team was actually shipping out to Iraq for our special mission.

Simultaneously, my wife and I were horrified when my wife was notified that her Army Reserve unit was being activated because of the war. We just had a baby, I was about to ship out to war, my grandmother had just died, and now my wife's reserve unit was activated and she had no idea where she might be sent off to. Because of this, my wife had to quit her job as a teacher, and she was trying to deal with a 4-month old infant while trying to get to her new Army unit on Ft Carson at five in the morning every day, and meanwhile I was locked down for mission planning and preparation for a deployment to war. This was a very stressful time for us and finally, the day came when it was time for me to go.

The day I left for the Iraq war was an unforgettable moment in my life. My wife was sitting in a rocking chair in the small room on the second floor of our modest house. Sunlight was streaming through the window so intensely that dust particles were visible in the air. The light splashed off our used crib and produced a silver sheen where it reflected off my wife's black hair and the pine bookcase I built for my daughter before she was born. My daughter was writhing and crying incessantly in my wife's lap as she struggled patiently to nurse her. There were tears running down my wife's face as I said goodbye. I kissed them both, my wife's tears wet my lips, I turned my back, and walked out; leaving everything in the world up to her to deal with alone...yet again. For some reason, in hindsight, I strongly remember turning my back on them, and every time I recall that moment my heart freezes for a moment.

I don't think I realized as much as my wife did, that I was actually leaving to go fight in a war, so there was a real chance that I would die in Iraq. That instant, that nanosecond prior to me turning my back, could have been the last time I ever saw them and they saw me. My wife didn't even know exactly where I was going, and there was no way to know how long I'd be gone if I ever came back at all. It's interesting how the choices we make in life can suddenly accumulate at singular events that define us, but only if we choose to reflect on them.

I walked down the stairs, slung my green duffel bag, took a deep breath, and mentally prepared myself to walk out the door.

# Chapter 5
## Northern Iraq, PUK Sector, 2003
## Advanced Force Operations (AFO)

I walked out of the house with my green duffel bag on my shoulder and shut the door behind me. I could still barely hear my baby daughter's muffled crying from outside. I stood under my simple house's small covered porch in civilian clothes and took a deep breath of the cold Colorado air. I clenched my eyes and fists and tried to block out the crying and focus: I was on my way to war. I vaguely recognized that five seconds before might have been the last time I would ever see my wife and daughter. I shrugged it all off and drove onto Ft. Carson, ultimately on my way to Iraq.

My team was chosen to perform Advanced Force Operations (AFO); a special type of mission that precedes Unconventional Warfare (UW) and pours the foundation for its success. UW is when Green Berets infiltrate denied areas to rally resistance forces and overthrow governments or terrorist groups. The goal of our AFO mission was to infiltrate Iraq undetected, link up with Kurdish resistance and the CIA, discover the Kurdish resistance forces' composition and disposition, and prepare to receive and integrate the rest of our Special Forces units into the war. There were also two other critical tasks. One was to register "shock and awe" targets against Ansar Al Islam (AAI) and the Iraqi military units along the "Green Line." The other was to repair the airstrip west of As Sulaymaniya, so our brethren would have a place to land. These missions were highly critical to the overarching war strategy.

## One Green Beret

I was about to become part of Task Force Viking, which would later become historically significant, if not legendary, within CIA and Special Forces circles.

Soon enough, my team and I landed at an Airbase in Turkey. We had travel orders that legitimized our arrival and purported that we were there for some uneventful training. Soon after landing, we met some mysterious folks from the CIA Special Activities Division, and they told us minimally what we needed to know and do to get ready for our infiltration. We stayed in guest housing as if we were on some routine visit.

The second day we were there, my company commander -a highly intelligent and soft-spoken man- along with some others from the "B-Team," arrived at the guest housing with a line of rental vehicles of random types and colors. They had rented the vehicles as part of applying for a "day pass" at the Air Force base, and they took whatever the rental company had. Of course, we had no intention of ever returning the vehicles to the rental car company since we were going to drive them into Iraq; these rental cars were our official infiltration platform, and we laughed about the day pass.

I was assigned a Jeep Cherokee, and my team also had a red low rider pickup with tinted windows. We all thought the low rider truck was hilarious. The vehicles smelled like cigarettes and had a stuffy feel to them.

I spent most of that day preparing my gear; we loaded magazines, packed ammo, secured hand grenades, and figured out how to hide our guns in the rental vehicles. We waited until dark to load the vehicles so no one else in the guest housing would be able to see us pack our weapons and ammunition under the seats and load our other baggage into the various vehicles.

We packed so that we'd be able to pass a shallow cursory check if we were inspected at the border. I was under the impression that if we were to get arrested or detained while trying to cross the border then we would have to fend for ourselves.

The next morning my heart raced anxiously as I got into the driver's seat of my vehicle, which was loaded with hidden weapons and equipment. It was cold, cloudy, and drizzling. I was wearing civilian clothes and a concealed pistol under my jacket. I felt like I was standing at the start point to a marathon or something; my anxiety was tinged with a bit of fear as I pondered all the things that might go wrong at the border, and all the consequences of those things.

I started the Jeep and drove among the small convoy of wacky, weapon laden rental vehicles boldly towards the Airbase's gate, beyond which lied an infinity of unknowns. We showed our day pass to the guards at the Airbase's gate, and we chuckled as they waved us through with bored looks on their faces; they had no idea we were about to drive all the way across Turkey and into Iraq.

We drove primarily across the southern part of Turkey towards Iraq in what would soon be considered missing rental cars. I began to fully realize the magnitude of the situation; we had just embarked on a low visibility infiltration into a denied country to spearhead an operation that would organize resistance forces, overthrow a government, knock out a major terrorist cell, and bring in hundreds of Green Berets to start a war. I had finally made it to the mission that every Green Beret trains for, and dreams of.

We were told to be at Habur gate, a border gate that separates Turkey from Iraq, during a very specific time window. I didn't know where we were supposed to go after we crossed into Iraq, how long it would take to get anywhere, or any other details.

After about an hour of tenuous driving, my nerve endings blasted my body with a tingling sensation in fear as a Turkish police car approached rapidly from behind with its lights flashing. To my relief the police car passed us and then turned in front of our small convoy. I became nervous again when the police car *stayed* in front of us, blue lights still on, and I wondered if someone had somehow organized an escort.

I should have been a lot more scared. We looked like a team of burly professional athletes, all male between the ages of 25 to 35, almost all of us could bench press over 250 pounds and run a half marathon at a moment's notice, and we wore the style of clothes that are typically worn by military men that are off duty. Not to mention, if anyone inspected our vehicles, they would have found an arsenal. I thought that if the Turkish policeman at the border discovered us then we would end up in Turkish prison. If we were caught on the border on the Iraqi side, I just hoped that it was all Kurds and that whoever we encountered would be "friendly." I have heard the saying "Hope is not a strategy" before, but in this case, hope was *our only strategy* as we inched our way towards the Iraqi border.

The drive through Turkey was long and dreary due to the weather; I didn't see anything other than razor wire and minefield signs along the Syrian border until we reached far enough east. After a while the foothills of the large mountains along the Iraq border materialized in the distance. We stopped to refuel twice.

## One Green Beret

During one stop at a tiny run-down gas station, a crowd of about ten or so skinny and dirty men with dark hair formed around me. Most of the men crouched while they smoked cigarettes, and they watched us like we were creatures from another world. One man approached me slowly, and he intently examined my face from less than a foot away, as if he was trying to figure out if I was real or not; I could smell his pungent body odor. I smiled, said hi, and patted him on the shoulder to put the man at ease; he flashed me a mostly toothless grin and walked away a bit embarrassed. I was careful not to make it apparent that I was armed because I didn't know how the Turkish police officer, who had stopped at the gas station with us, would act if he saw a weapon on one of us. I didn't know if he knew who we really were. It was still raining, at times sleeting, and extremely cold.

As I drove along and perceived the scenery before me, I realized that Eastern Turkey is a very rough place. On the last gas stop we made, I saw an entire hillside that looked like a massive pile of mud with sparse grass and the occasional ledge poking out. There were tiny black cave entrances like pockmarks all over it, some of which had satellite dishes mounted in makeshift fashions outside of them and people were squatting or sitting in the mud in the rain outside of the holes. After some subconscious deliberation, I concluded that the holes were their homes. I waved to them and some of them waved back. As we continued driving east, in my mind I wished them all the best. Eastern Turkey made Kosovo look like a five-star hotel, and Bosnia like the Taj Mahal.

As we neared the border, my captain received a call from our people on the other side of the border via satellite phone; they had been there for several months. We were on track for arrival, and apparently they had given my Captain some specific instructions that filtered down to me as "just keep driving when you get there," so I just kept driving the Jeep Cherokee forward. I felt intense anxiety growing in the pit of my stomach. It felt like that day I rode the turret into the center of the UCPMB base camp in Kosovo, except this time it was me who was driving, and the magnitude of this situation was much greater.

Once we were close to the border, and many slow hours had passed, we turned a corner through a large mud puddle in the road and suddenly I saw five or six camera crews filming us drive by! My mind raced and nerves perked, and a flurry of questions streamed through my mind: Who was filming us and why? Had we been caught? Was our whole mission compromised? How did they know we were coming? Will we end up in Turkish prison? Who did they think they were filming? Do they know we are a US Special Forces team? How do I escape? Should we kill them? I quickly realized that I had no choice but to just keep driving and keep hoping, so that's what I did. My anxiety diminished, but only slightly, as I distanced myself from the scene but got closer to the border.

The sun went down, and it was still raining as we approached the lights of Habur gate; the entrance to Iraq. As we neared the border, I thought of the infiltration phase of "Robin Sage" (the epic Green Beret training exercise) and compared it to what I was going though. Instead of being in the back of a truck with a tarp thrown over me in the hills of North Carolina, I was in a rental car approaching Iraq, and I was wearing a North Face jacket and pants with a concealed pistol instead of an Army uniform.

For no particular reason, my expectation was that Habur gate would be like that small makeshift gate the UCPMB had constructed in Kosovo. However, the image of that rickety wooden gate in Velja Glava was obliterated as I peered through the foggy windshield at what looked like the lights from a sprawling built-up area. Scattered ambient light from a multitude of windows and streetlights emulated from the central area of the gate and made the whole dark and muddled scene before me glow as we approached in the misty darkness.

As we crept towards the inner part of the gate, the stress increased, my heart was pounding super hard, and I had no idea what was going to happen. We were all completely silent as I drove the car slowly and relentlessly forward...painstakingly *forward*. I felt like I had succumbed to the gravitational pull of a black hole. The border was a great analogy for the event horizon, because I was either going to die or cross over, and once we crossed there was no turning back. I had one hand on the steering wheel, and I put my locked-and-loaded pistol under my left thigh, so it was accessible from between my legs, but still hidden.

I definitively decided that I was not going to Turkish prison under any circumstances. I was prepared to fight my way into Iraq or die trying. I decided that there was no other option.

The tension in my body steadily increased as we approached the final place where I thought we would cross the international border into Iraq. It was very dark, and my vision was annoyingly blurry. The brake lights on the vehicle in front of me came on, and then the rough image of a Turkish soldier or policeman, I couldn't tell which, materialized in the murky darkness, rain, and dim light. He had oppressively low hanging clouds behind him that reflected eerie grey light downwards from the expansive dark sky. He signaled repetitively for me to continue, like a cop at a traffic circle. I slipped into a robotic state; there was nothing I could do but drive forward until I was told to stop, and if the Turks tried to stop us then it was go-time. The Turkish cop was on the driver's side of the car when I drove the vehicle past him, and I got the impression from his gestures and the look of strain on his face that he was scared. I wondered frantically if he was directing us to a holding area where our vehicle would be inspected, in which case we'd have been instantly compromised, and my stress and heart rate accelerated even more at the thought as I prepared to react.

We passed the guard, and then suddenly stopped in a narrow area under a bit of overhead cover behind the rest of the convoy. I pondered what had just happened with the Turkish official who just waved us through: Did he know what we were doing there, and who we were, but the Turks were ok with it? Why was that police car driving with us most of the time? I quickly realized that I didn't have any answers to questions like this by design. I wasn't supposed to know, none of my assumptions could be confirmed nor questions answered, so I settled on the reality that I didn't need to know any of this anyway. I only needed to listen to my leadership; I trusted them with my life without question. My Captain said to drive forward. That's what I did.

Several of us got out of the car and used a bathroom in an exotically decorated building. The toilets were Middle Eastern hole in the floor style, and there were bright colors, intricate turnings, and stenciling everywhere in the building I went into. Everything seemed very poorly lit, as if there was a veil of darkness and obscurity over everything around me.

As soon as I returned from the bathroom, I got back in the driver's seat and continued onward. Within a few minutes we left the confines of the Habur gate area, and the road started to open up a bit. Through the rain and darkness, my headlights barely provided me the ability to perceive some rather stubby trees along the sides of the road. My Captain told us over the radio that we had officially entered Iraq, and we were headed towards our first linkup with members of a CIA "Ground Branch" team, our unit's "pilot team," and some Kurdish KDP members. The "ground branch" CIA team was a CIA Special Activities Division team, and a Pilot team is a Green Beret team that focuses on preparatory activities related to UW. In my foggy rear-view mirror, I saw the lights of Habur gate fade in the distance through the mist and rain, and we continued deeper into Iraq.

After a few more minutes, we all stopped again along the side of a narrow road lined with small trees, some Kurds got out of vehicles along with some CIA folks, and they all went to my Captain's vehicle. These Kurds were part of the KDP, and they were the first Kurds I had ever seen in my life. The rays of light from my headlights fought the oppressive rain and darkness just sufficiently enough that I could see they were surprisingly clean-cut; thin forms in camouflage uniforms with short dark hair and prominent noses, some wore military style hats. The Kurds told us that the Iraqi Military knew we had arrived, and therefore we needed to travel outside the range of Iraqi "Green Line" artillery and rockets. They told us to follow them the way they suggested, which was to traverse the foothills of the immense mountains along the Turkish border towards our unknown final destination, which was somewhere near As Sulaymaniyah. We had already driven almost all the way across Turkey, but we still had a very long way to go – all the way across Northern Iraq.

The Kurds went back to their vehicles and so did my Captain. I depressed the accelerator again and we continued moving forward. We followed the Kurds along rough winding roads until it was evident even in the pitch blackness that we had climbed up into the mountains. My ears popped several times, and over the course of a few hours the rain turned to sleet, the sleet turned to snow, and as we climbed even higher it was snowing sideways. Huge snowflakes sparkled in my headlights as I struggled to look through the foggy windshield, and for a long time we were in complete whiteout conditions. We were at the complete mercy of the Kurds who were escorting us and had really no choice but to trust them.

I didn't even know where we were *generally* located at any point in time because our GPS was not working. We were moving so slowly through the snowy mountains that periodically Kurds *walked past* my vehicle as it inched along in the whiteout. A few times, the Kurds stood at key places along the roads or trails in order to make sure no one drove off the road and perhaps off a massive cliff. At some point, Kurdish men actually led our ragbag convoy of rental cars on foot because the visibility was so bad due to the snow.

We drove precariously in this fashion almost all night long, through relentlessly winding and brutal mountain roads and trails. Keeping the windows defogged was nearly impossible, and my vision continued to frustrate me. Nothing at all was visible outside of the cones of light from my headlights, and the cones of light were almost completely full of sparkling white snowflakes. We refueled from gas cans that the Kurds had in their trucks, which were up near the front of the small convoy.

## One Green Beret

I was falling asleep at the wheel when we finally broke out of the mountains and it stopped snowing. After a few hours we pulled into a "safe house" somewhere north of Irbil or Mosul somewhere. I got out of the vehicle and looked around. It was a tremendously austere site, surrounded by those stubby trees. Some KDP personnel shuffled us to a rectangular white concrete block building. They spoke Kurdish to each other, so I didn't understand them. Their mannerisms were welcoming, generous, and polite. The simple building had one room and no heat, and just a thin carpet on a rough poured concrete floor. There was a musty smell in the air inside the room and we all piled in.

It had been 27 hours since we left the Air Force base in Turkey on our 24-hour day pass. I spoke to some of the CIA guys and the Pilot Team very briefly, but it was obvious they were not supposed to tell us very much, or we were all just too tired to talk. Even though I was exhausted from the drive and the stress, it was impossible to get any quality sleep. I just laid there in silence. I couldn't believe I was actually in Iraq, and I had no idea where I was. As I laid there, I thought about my newborn baby daughter, the horrible situation I had left my wife with, and the memories of my amazing grandma who had just died shortly before I left, and I figured they'd be proud of us.

The plan for the next morning (only a few hours later since it was already morning) was to drive to a place referred to as "painted rock," which was on the notional border that separated the PUK and KDP portions of Iraqi Kurdistan. I knew the PUK and KDP did not get along, so I could only hope this linkup would go well. There were tribal, political, and many other historical reasons why there was so much tension between the

KDP and PUK, but we just had to survive the linkup at painted rock and continue our mission with the PUK.

I thanked the KDP members, and we loaded into our vehicles again. We took off and followed the KDP and CIA guys in a generally south-easterly direction towards As Sulaymaniyah.

Along the way, there were very few trees anywhere, and the mostly green landscape was massive in scale. To my front right, green rolling hills with exposed ledge mixed with grass extended until fading out to an endless brown expanse that met the horizon. To the north I perceived an enormity of snowcapped peaks that commanded the same degree of respect as the Rocky Mountains did back in Colorado. The sky was uniquely large and foreboding.

As we neared Painted Rock, I realized that it was literally an area along the road where the rocks and exposed ledge were painted many different colors. These wild colored rocks comprised my first introduction to the PUK, a very colorful culture that I learned to appreciate and respect forever. We stopped the vehicles at a sizable washed-out dirt area on the side of the road at painted rock and waited for a while. My captain and the CIA guys stood a few meters away, talking on the satellite phone.

Within an hour of sitting in the cold Jeep, I saw a convoy of vehicles in the distance to the east. The convoy approached along the crude, pothole covered windy road that squirmed through the grassy hills and ledge. The convoy consisted of SUVs and other cars of many colors, and they were sandwiched between two small Nissan pickup trucks with soviet .50 caliber machine guns mounted on them. The PUK Kurds pulled up and started getting out of the vehicles, and I instantly took notice at the vast difference between the uniformed appearances of the KDP as opposed to the PUK members. This was the first time I had actually seen any PUK Kurds, the *Peshmerga* so they're called, and they looked exactly like the way I imagined a true guerilla fighting force would look; I liked them instantly.

They all wore extremely baggy and somewhat tapered dark Khaki pants made of heavy material (which we instantly deemed *MC Hammer pants* due to the similarity). They had AK 47s and other weapons that looked like they had been "bedazzled." They had checkered black and white head wraps, tennis shoes, and some of them had flowers sewn into the knit covers that encapsulated the ammunition drums on their AKs. Some had fancy pistols tucked into their light tan cloth belts that they wrapped around their waists (which also served at tourniquets for injuries when needed), and they all had big moustaches, big smiles, and a lot of confidence and intelligence in their powerful eyes.

The KDP and PUK folks shouted to each other in Kurdish in what seemed like very gruff and awkward ways, as if this hand-off was something that they both wanted to get over with as quickly as possible. After their brief exchange, the KDP departed, and we were left with the PUK guys. Two Green Berets who I hadn't seen in months from back in Colorado jumped out of one of the SUVs that had just arrived with the PUK convoy; they were members of my battalion's Pilot Team (one of them had been on our team previously).

They wore Kurdish clothing with their US weapons and ammo vests on top. The Pilot Team's Team Sergeant looked hilarious: a white guy with a barely-under-control auburn afro, wearing Oakley sunglasses, with an auburn 1970s moustache, in his MC Hammer pants and PUK shirt, and a combat vest and M4 carbine slung across his chest. We all man-hugged, they complimented us on our red tinted window low rider rental truck, laughed at the fact that the cars might now be officially missing back in Turkey, we laughed at their MC Hammer pants, and we got a quick brief about the threats in the area. It was no more than two or three minutes before we piled back into the vehicles.

The Pilot Team told us that we should always travel between PUK machine gun trucks due to the threat from Ansar Al Islam (AAI), Islamic Group of Kurdistan (IGK), Islamic Movement of Kurdistan (IMK), and the Kurdish Workers Party (PKK) terrorist groups, as well as Iranian, Iraqi, and Syrian Intelligence threats operating throughout the PUK area. I was stunned by the number of threats, and a persistent feeling of tenseness settled in.

We shook some PUK hands, and then hit the road again. We drove for several more hours. Along the way, I looked south across the terrain towards the "Green Line" out of the right side of the vehicle. The Green Line followed a physical ridge in most places, so it looked like someone drew a crooked line across the entire southern horizon, and it made an interesting backdrop to an almost infinite expanse of green and rocky terrain we were driving through. In some areas along the Green Line, I saw bunkers and radio towers and other indications of Iraqi military presence. We were definitely in the enemy's back yard, because the Green Line was where two thirds of the Iraqi Army were positioned as a "front line" facing north against Iraqi Kurdistan, a foreboding sight to me as one of a handful of Green Berets who were on their own with no support in a completely unknown place. Looking at the Green Line and all those enemy Iraqi troops gave me the chills. The endless Iraqi military positions made me feel like an underdog as we drove east for several more hours.

When we finally approached the outskirts of As Sulaymaniyah it was so dark I could only perceive it as a cluster of sprawling lights in the distance, which made it look like a giant hovering spacecraft due to the sheer blackness of the backdrop. We took a bypass road around the west side of As Sulaymaniyah that led north towards a village called Qual A Challan, which I soon learned was our final destination.

As we passed As Sulaymaniyah It dawned on me again that we had absolutely no external support from anyone whatsoever; no medical evacuation possible, no air support, no ex-filtration, nothing. So, if we were injured or killed by one of the terrorist groups in the area, or if the Kurds turned on us, or the Iraqis attacked the Kurds (all these situations were considered possible to varying degrees), we were on our own. We had an "evasion plan," but realistically if anything other than a catastrophic loss of rapport with the Kurds happened, we were going to stay and fight to the death alongside the PUK. If the PUK turned on us, and we survived for longer than an instant (unlikely), we would have to escape and evade using any means necessary. As Green Berets we accepted conditions such as these without issue.

Finally, we arrived near Qual A Challan where the CIA and the Pilot Team (which acted as a single unit) lived in a cluster of houses. They helped us settle into a different house. Our house had very expensive tile floors, tall ceilings, and it was surrounded by a high brick fence. I cordially greeted a few of the Peshmerga who were outside guarding us and thanked them for doing so. We unloaded the vehicles and organized our equipment and started to talk about how we were going to operate in sectors.

The CIA Branch Chief gave us a warm welcome; he called himself Uncle Andy. He was a retired marine turned CIA operative, and we met the rest of his team. Most of them were former special operators of some kind. Uncle Andy gave us a very thorough briefing about the situation in our area of responsibility, and I was amazed by the area's complexity. The CIA people that briefed us were surprised that my team had not been given any of the intelligence they had reported prior to our infiltration. It would have taken weeks to fully comprehend and digest the richness and nuance of the information they had collected. It was a shame that no one ever really saw that information.

After Uncle Andy's overview, we then met several of the key Kurdish leaders, including Bafel Talibani. Bafel was the son of Jalal Talibani – the leader of the PUK, and future president of Iraq. I acquired a genuine PUK uniform, complete with MC Hammer pants, head wrap, and a button-down shirt with "P.U.K." embroidered on it. We wore these until the war started, so when we drove around, we blended in better (at least from a distance). There was a satellite TV in our house, so we watched the news to see how the situation was developing. One day I watched someone on the news deny that the US had anyone in Iraq yet.

*My PUK Uniform (photo is mine)*

After we decided our sectors, I was in charge of figuring out where we should integrate our Alpha Company into the Kurdish units once they arrived (whenever the war actually started). My sector spanned the territory between As Sulaymaniya all the way up to Taq Taq and then north along the boundary between the PUK and KDP, all the way to Turkey and Iran. Taq Taq was almost on the Green Line, and at the western most edge of the PUK area.

My sector was an enormous area, I would guess around 5000 square kilometers. I remember standing about 6 feet away from the giant map we had taped to the wall, and my area looked like an imperceptible mass. Some of the areas of my sector took five or six hours to reach by vehicle from Qual A Challan. I really didn't know where to begin, and I had to figure out where 6 Teams would live and operate when they arrived, and I didn't have a lot of time. The other guys on my team formed sub teams and had other sectors with responsibility to bring in our (3$^{Rd}$ Battalion) B and C companies.

The most important sector for sure was not mine, it was the area east of Halabja where the Ansar Al Islam (AAI) radical Islamic group controlled a very large and brutally mountainous area against the Iranian border. The Islamic Group of Kurdistan (IGK), and the Islamic Movement of Kurdistan (IMK) groups also operated there, and both of their territories were connected to the north and south borders of the AAI enclave, respectively. During random conversations with the Peshmerga about AAI (the Kurds are Muslim) over tea, I learned that radical Islam is not Islam at all; radical "islamists" are just gangs of psychos that generate ridiculous interpretations of religion to use as excuses for their behavior. AAI had a poison and chemical production facility in a small village called Sargat, which is near a village called Khurmal. We would deal with them soon enough (next chapter).

Once the CIA and Pilot team provided my team a sufficient level of situational awareness, we started working our sectors as best we could. I drove, with two Peshmerga machine gun trucks for security and my SUV in the middle, out to my sector almost every day with the goal of collecting details about the disparate Peshmerga units, and trying to find the best places for our brethren teams to stay when they arrived. It was difficult to know where to go; the maps we had did not reflect the nuances of reality at all. The Peshmerga gave us tips of where to go and helped us get there. Without them we would have been ineffective, and we wouldn't have been safe traveling around. It was also difficult simply because of the distances we had to drive to find various PUK groups. Some days I drove for 8 or 10 hours, just to meet a single group of Peshmerga in a village somewhere for an hour or so to see what was there. Often when we arrived at various places (dozens of places) we were disappointed to discover that there weren't many fighters there, or they lacked weapons, or the village wouldn't have been suitable for one of our teams to operate from. We also only had one real interpreter, so as a team we couldn't easily explore the whole PUK area simultaneously.

Managing all the data we collected on our computers, and digitally transmitting that data back to our headquarters was very challenging. None of us were technology professionals, so managing large amounts of photos that linked to documents was frustrating and error prone. Also, the technology at the time was not as capable as it is today. Moreover, we were using a certain type of radio that made it difficult to transmit large files, like photos. We tried to transmit every couple of days, and sometimes it took dozens of attempts and many hours to get the information back. The information that *did* make it back was difficult for the guys on the other end to piece together because we had to break all the files into pieces, and then send the pieces over different transmissions. Therefore, hyperlinks didn't work, document and photos were hard to put into context, and ultimately the information we sent was very hard for the recipients to consume.

Due to these challenges, we were afraid we wouldn't get our job done before the war kicked off. It was nerve-racking to say the least. It was also at times frustrating because I had unrealistic expectations for what the Kurds would tell us.

On one occasion, during one of the long trips into my sector, my colleague and I encountered a band of PUK fighters that numbered in the hundreds. For each element of Peshmerga that we discovered, we always asked them a few standard questions about their capabilities and disposition. We needed to know what the Kurds would do if the Iraqis invaded Kurdistan, and if such an invasion happened, we needed to know which areas would be protected by which Kurdish groups. This one experience, near the village of Taq Taq, was a good lesson in the simplicity and effectiveness of the PUK Peshmerga groups.

As I approached this PUK unit's compound, at the end of a muddy dirt road surrounded by rolling hills, a large group of armed Peshmerga with thick mustaches, MC Hammer pants, and black and white checkered head wraps started to materialize and become clearer through the light fog. They gathered around our vehicle as I depressed the brakes, and I heard them murmuring curiously in Kurdish. I opened the door and stepped out slowly. Since I was wearing a PUK uniform, but I obviously wasn't Kurdish, they looked at me cautiously. I waved and smiled to make sure they realized I was friendly, and I asked if I could speak to the leader of their group. A man raised his hand and stepped forward, he was 5 foot 8 or so, probably in his 50s. He had very intelligent and intense eyes, wore the classic Kurdish pants as well as a combat vest full of AK magazines, and his AK was slung on his shoulder. We shook hands and exchanged greetings, and I walked a few meters with him into a block building and we sat down on the thin carpet that covered the concrete floor. A younger Kurd brought us tea and I thanked him respectfully. I asked the leader of this group, like I had many other leaders of many other small groups in the previous weeks, via our interpreter, a series of questions that amounted to a dialog something like this:

"If the Iraqis attack, then what areas would your group protect and operate in?"

"We will *attack* them wherever they are" he answered calmly, but he stirred and seemed a bit confused by this question and tried to be respectful with his answer, then I countered again.

"Well, if you attack them *there* and they flank you, who will attack the flanking Iraqi element?"

He stirred a bit more, and his eyes narrowed a bit

"...We will just attack them on the flank as well...and anywhere else they are...and if we need more Peshmerga, then inshallah they will come."

After making some small talk with this Peshmerga leader for a few minutes, we were done, and I went back outside. I shook a few hands on the way to our vehicle, and within a few minutes we were on our way back to Qual A Challan. This encounter taught me that the Peshmerga did not really embrace defense as a strategy. The Peshmerga specialize in *offense*, even as a means of defense. The US military thinks very mechanically about combat operations and tactics, and my expectation was to hear similar mechanics from the Peshmerga. This was a senseless expectation to have, and I would see very soon how effective the Kurds were in real combat.

After many instances of conversations like the one I just described with various tribes and villages and militia units over the course of the next month or so, I kind of settled into the routine of the mission. It was actually very similar in nature to the JCO Missions. We incrementally built a depiction of where the PUK had fighters, where those fighters could and would operate, and what kind of weapons they had or could acquire. We continued to find which areas were most suitable to become the places where the incoming Green Beret teams would live once they arrived and the war started. The incoming teams needed to be located in areas of tactical significance, where they could best assist the most Kurdish units and have the best access to infrastructure such as electricity, water, roads, and places to buy necessities. So, we spent the next month doing an "Unconventional Warfare Assessment" in which the goal was to depict where all the Kurds were, and find a suitable home for each of our incoming teams. I had paper notes stuck all over that big paper wall map.

Repairing the As Sulaymaniya West Airstrip so that it was operational again was one of the most important tasks of our AFO mission. We had infiltrated Iraq with an Air Force Special Tactics Squadron (STS) guy, along with about $320,000.00 cash in order to pay Kurdish construction workers to fix the runway. The STS guy was there as an operator on our team, to certify the runway, and direct aircraft once the war started. We needed to fix the runway so MC-130s could bring the rest of our Green Beret brothers into the fight when the war officially started.

Soon my team leadership decided that we might fail our mission if we stayed in Qual A Challan; it just took too long to get anywhere from there, we were short on interpreters, and the prolonged exposure on the roads was too risky because the Kurds had information that AAI planned to attack us via vehicular suicide bombings and drive-by tactics. So, we planned to move to the Peshmerga Headquarters that was a few miles west of the As Sulaymaniyah Airstrip to decrease travel time and risks, and to be closer to the work being done on the Airstrip.

A few days later we moved down to the Kurdish Headquarters near As Sulaymaniyah West (ASW). Since we basically "lived off the land" in the modern sense of the phrase, it was very easy to move from place to place. It was here at ASW that we became even more integrated into the daily life of the Peshmerga. We got to know key Kurdish leaders, and they took great care of us. I was reminded of my times in Bosnia, living among the local people and realizing how amazing they are. The PUK built us showers, and they even acquired "regular" toilets for us, even though they really didn't understand what we thought was so great about them. We met soldiers' families and got to know and love the Kurdish culture. I spoke German to one of the commanders all the time, his eye had been shot out by AAI a few months prior near Halabja. He was like my personal interpreter at times, and we liked to talk about the differences between what I saw in Kurdistan vice what it was like in America. The minister of defense equivalent to the PUK also spoke German, so my Captain and I were able to communicate well with him. Both my Captain and I were quite proficient in German, we had "fluency" according to the Defense Language Proficiency Test (DLPT). Since it's common for Kurds to perform migrant work in Germany many of them spoke some German. This allowed us to talk to quite a few people without an interpreter, which was very handy. It was especially useful when the Minister of defense and other Kurdish leaders wanted to speak to us in private sometimes.

We almost always ate dinner with them. They put all the food in big trays on a high table, and everyone just stood around the table and dug into the trays to fill their plate, usually with large spoons. The women never ate with us, but there always seemed to be a few of them peeking out from the kitchen area, probably just wanting to see what an American looked like. I adapted and grew quite fond of Kurdish life; the fried grass, the outstanding tea, the baklava, and the unbelievable strength and kindness. The fried grass was a bit prickly, but we got used to it, and it became a favorite of mine. The tea was usually red, and the Kurds served it in small vase-like glass cups that were about three or four inches high and an inch in diameter. They put very raw sugar in the bottom of each glass, and we would stir in as much as we wanted as they filled and refilled the elegant little cups.

There were hundreds, possibly thousands of Peshmerga in ASW, and it was only a twenty-minute drive to the airfield and an hour to get into my sector. We were able to cover way more of our area of responsibility at a much faster pace. Our productivity increased by the day, and so did our rapport with the Peshmerga.

One day, four members of the IMK, whose enclave was adjacent to AAI's eastern flank, attacked ASW; the PUK killed them all before they even got near the gate. When I heard the gunfire just a few hundred meters away I became hyper aware of our situation. This incident made it official that these extremist groups knew we were there, and they wanted us dead. The PUK told us there were bounties on our heads, and that there had even been pictures of us distributed somehow, kind of like "Wanted" posters from the Wild West.

As the threat of IMK, IGK, and AAI increased in the area, we began to treat our Air Force guy like a VIP; if he was killed, who would validate the runway, and how would the rest of our unit get there if the runway was untrustworthy? I was put in charge of working with the Kurdish security folks to make sure they had what they needed to implement the right security controls at ASW.

One day out of nowhere we were told via our satellite phone, that four Iraqi MIG fighter jets had just taken off from near Baghdad and they were headed north. I translated "headed north" into "coming to kill us." I immediately assumed they were headed towards our location on a bombing run to take us out as a preemptive strike. One of the Iraqi's potential courses of action was to launch a "Hail Mary" attack into Northern Iraq against the Kurds; possibly a *chemical* attack. Remember that Saddam did gas the Kurds in Halabja in 1988, so the threat was real. We immediately informed the Kurds, we all ran away from the building and spread out as much as possible, and we made sure we had our gas masks. While I was lying in the grass a few hundred meters from the building, nerves throbbing and heart slapping my t-shirt, anxiously and fearfully listening for the sound of incoming jets, I wondered what they would tell my wife if I died at that moment. Luckily, the jets never arrived, but this was another stark reminder of how isolated we were.

Before long I had collected and reported all the info I could for my sector, and we as a team had sufficiently finished figuring out where all the Kurds *were*. I had walked through minefields with Kurds to get better vantage points on the Iraqis to collect grid coordinates of critical Iraqi positions. I saw large piles of human feces in remote sites along the green line because there were no facilities, but hundreds of Kurds were staged there. I saw PKK positions in the distance along the Turkish border. I saw a red-haired Kurd blow bubbles into his motorcycle gas tank with a large straw to mix the fuel and then take off for the Green Line to collect information for us. I was denied a handshake and told to leave one village because the US had left the Kurds hanging back in the 90s. I saw an infinite amount of amazing courage and cunning in the Kurds while discovering their composition and disposition (with extensive help from my leadership). Finally, in mid-March 2003, we finalized the As Sulaymaniyah airstrip and our Air Force guy gave it his official blessing, and we knew where we were going to place all the incoming teams.

It was the second half of March and we still didn't know when the rest of the Green Berets in my unit would arrive, nor when the war would actually start. Turkey still wouldn't let anyone in, and I was feeling very stranded and isolated; one of a handful of Green berets and CIA guys, embedded with the Peshmerga for over two months. We went to Jalal Talabani's (the future president of Iraq and leader of the PUK) house near the Dukan dam and briefed him on our plans. I wasn't personally involved in the meeting, but according to my Captain, "Mam Jalal" thought we were doing ok.

While we waited for "higher" to tell us when the war was going to start, we shifted our focus to targeting AAI. We made many trips into Halabja, which was very near where AAI operated. Halabja was on the outskirts of the brownish green foothills of the massive snowcapped peaks along the Iranian border. Every time we approached the area, AAI spotted our small groups of SUVs, and they launched rocket and mortar attacks against us and the Peshmerga headquarters. On one such occasion, a Kurd was killed by the tailfin of a katoosha rocket that had screamed in and exploded several yards away. This was the first time I had heard incoming mortars and rockets...they don't whistle...they sound more like the whoosh of a small airplane, but faster.

We performed repetitive reconnaissance operations on the border of AAI's territory to register targets for the shock and awe campaign. I spent a lot of time sitting behind a high-powered spotting scope with a CIA guy on the edge of AAI's territory. He wrote down coordinates as I plotted with a laser range finder. We registered anything we saw that looked like it might be a defensive position or a place where AAI fighters might consolidate.

At one point, the PUK made some kind of deal (that I was unaware of) with the IGK that permitted us to enter into IGK territory to get a better look at AAI, because inside IGK territory we would have several great vantage points on AAI. Once the arrangement was solidified, three of us, along with one CIA guy, drove nervously through IGK's dusty entrance gate. I was incredibly tense as we passed several IGK heavy machine gun positions that were manned by bearded, dirty fighters who wore ragged tan combat gear as well as wide black headbands with white Arabic writing on them. My nervousness spiked as the men glared at us with an unsettling, calm intensity. IGK had no idea that we were not only there to register shock and awe targets against AAI, but we were *also* there to register shock and awe targets against *them*. I captured waypoints on my GPS as we drove past more machine gun positions, and others took notes on azimuths and distances from the waypoints so we could later produce coordinates of key positions. We were deep inside IGK territory for several hours, registered several key AAI targets from relatively concealed locations, and then drove back out the same way we came in.

As part of our shock and awe targeting efforts against AAI, I spent one night in a snowstorm on a hilltop, next to a dead Kurd and a CIA guy, receiving sporadic mortar fire from AAI, with no overhead protection, in a wet sleeping bag. Such is the life of a Green Beret.

We also continued to register Iraqi military locations along the Green Line for the shock and awe. On one occasion, we did a classic recon operation to identify key Iraqi positions along the Green Line. We geared up, had our rucksacks filled, and set out to occupy a ridgeline north of a village called Cham Chamal, which was very close to the Green Line. After our arrival, we set out on foot along a very large ridge as if we were sneaking around to avoid detection. However, we soon realized there were PUK guys everywhere, and they started asking us why we were carrying so much stuff. I guess they were curious as to where we could possibly be going that we would need so much. We quickly realized that even though we were only about a kilometer from the Iraqis, they could not distinguish us from the Kurds. The final tip that made me realize we were being silly was when a couple Kurds showed up with a platter of meats and a pot of tea. I quickly realized, greatly humbled, that we didn't need to recon anything; the Kurds already knew where all the Iraqi positions were, and what was at each one. They drew information onto the maps that we carried, and pointed out into the distance, describing in unbelievable detail what was along the Green Line, and *behind* the Green Line, which we were now casually observing from the ridgeline north of Cham Chamal as we sipped tea and ate meat off of a platter. I learned a lesson: The Kurds knew more than we would ever be able to learn by ourselves, and we learned to accept that fact and leverage it. We were not experts in war, *they were*, in fact I felt like an idiot when it came to war compared to the Peshmerga. The Peshmerga are a fighting force like no other.

I began to wonder if the war would ever start, and if the rest of my unit would ever arrive. However, in late March, apparently someone up the chain decided that it was time to use another option to get the rest of the Green Berets into Northern Iraq immediately; I guess the only option was to fly over enemy territory. I was notified at the last minute, when the aircraft were already on their way.

These daring flights, which carried two battalions of Green Berets over hostile territory, eventually became known as "The Ugly Baby." They flew the entire 2nd and 3rd Battalions of the 10th Special Forces group on the longest MC130 Talon combat flight in history, all the way from Jordan, over Iraq, and into Northern Iraq over significant anti-aircraft fire.

Some of my team stayed in Halabja, but I scrambled to get my gear together, and then I headed for the As Sulaymaniyah airstrip to handle the reception of our teams. Within a few hours, I stood on the edge of the ASW runway looking into the dark sky, and I overheard the intense fear-laden radio traffic from the pilots as they evaded anti-aircraft fire. We prepared buses to get the teams out to their designated locations so they could link up with their assigned Peshmerga units. Thousands of Kurds constituted a huge perimeter around the airstrip, and we blocked off every road including the main ones. No one was permitted to enter, and traffic got backed up for miles.

We set up lights along the runway so the aircraft would be able to identify it easier, and I listened to the pilots feverishly screaming status over the radio as they flew in the Ugly Baby. It was intense beyond imagination as I listened to their radio chatter. As per Murphy's law, as the Talons prepared for final approach, a Kurd accidentally fired an RPG into the air (it was slung on his shoulder facing up when it went off), and the generator that was running the lights on the runway died, resulting in a completely blacked-out airstrip. For a moment, the pilots questioned the security of the airstrip because of the RPG, and my leadership convinced them it was OK. I was glad that I was already on the ground.

The aircraft were shot to shit. Our Air Force STS guy had trouble vectoring the pilots onto the airstrip as they approached, so he employed an ingenious tactic. He jumped in the Jeep Cherokee and sped off down the runway to "lead the plane by the nose;" (his words) his plan was to drive the vehicle to the end of the airstrip, with the headlights on, and then drive back down towards where I was in order to give the pilots a reference point as they approached. I was confused as to why this was necessary, as I assumed that the pilots had night vision, but since the Air Force STS guy said it was required, I believed it because when it came to Aircraft, he was the ultimate authority.

I oversaw security on the ground for the Ugly Baby, and I was constantly talking to guys that we had embedded out on the roadblocks to report the situation from our flanks. There were thousands of cars backed up along every avenue of approach leading to the road that passed the Airstrip. The explosion from the accidental RPG round occurred at a time that we actually thought it might have been the Iraqis launching rockets from the Green Line. Anxiety was high, and the scale and significance of this historic operation are hard to overstate.

It was an incredible scene: an Air Force guy maniacally driving in front of a wounded MC130 aircraft down a newly repaired airstrip that we could only hope would hold up once the planes touched down on it. An RPG exploded and hundreds of Kurds chattered as they tried to get a look at my night vision goggles and day/night sniper scope on my rifle. I had constant situation reports streaming into my radio headset because hundreds of cars were now backed up on the roads leading in as people reported to me from the roadblocks, and Ltc Tovo kept asking me what was going on and if everything was secure. Truth be told, in hindsight I had no idea if anything was truly secure.

Finally, the aircraft screamed in and clattered noisily down the airstrip to where I was standing along with a few hundred Peshmerga. The two aircraft looked so huge and black that they appeared blacker than the darkness that surrounded them, the smell of fuel was alarming, and they were so loud and monstrous the crowd of curious Kurds instantly began to encircle them in awe, as if an alien spacecraft had landed. The plane was smoking from the damage it had incurred from taking fire during its journey over denied air space, and it was dripping fuel, which made us fearful of an explosion. The birds came to a complete stop, and the pilots lowered the tailgates. Dim reddish light spilled out of the tailgate onto the runway, and I perceived human forms run down the ramp and some knelt and kissed the ground. It was a harrowing flight to say the least. My feeling of isolation faded as I watched dozens of my fellow Green Berets unload. I expected to take rocket fire from the Iraqis, and I was surprised by their lack of response since there were thousands of them only a short distance away along the Green Line, and we were in rocket range.

We had prepared buses, as planned, to take the teams to the Kurdish villages that we had identified for them. The Kurds and I helped the incoming teams find the right buses to bring them to their respective Peshmerga hosts. I saw people that I hadn't seen in months from other teams and companies back in Colorado. They were surprised to see me because no one knew we were already in Iraq. We had prepared packets of information for each team, and the packets told them about the place they were going and the Peshmerga leadership they would link up with. I was stunned when one of the guys told me that they hadn't received any of the information we, the CIA, nor the Pilot team had reported the whole time we'd been there on AFO. Information and Intelligence flow had been an abysmal failure; the teams had absolutely no idea where they were going nor who their Kurdish militia leaders were. It was terrible, but like good Green Berets, they were accustomed to operating on little to no information for extended periods of time under extremely tenuous conditions, so they were all smiles, and ready to go wherever they needed to start making shit happen.

As the buses faded from view and the chaos subsided, the crowd of Kurds cleared and Ltc Tovo patted me on the back. I radioed to the roadblocks to let traffic flow again. I let out a massive sigh of relief. It was surreal. We had infiltrated Northern Iraq, linked up with the CIA, discovered where all the Kurds were, figured out where to put our teams, registered tons of shock and awe targets, and successfully infiltrated two battalions of Green Berets into Northern Iraq according to plan; the AFO mission was a success.

The war still hadn't officially started yet, and I left for Halabja to link up with the rest of my team to prepare for the assault on Ansar Al Islam, which would later become known as *Operation Viking Hammer*, the largest single Unconventional Warfare attack in the History of the Green Berets.

On the way down the road to Halabja in the dark morning hours, in the back seat of an SUV driving behind a Kurdish gun truck, my mind raced thinking about what I was about to encounter.

# Chapter 6
## Halabja area, Northern Iraq, 2003
## From the Ugly Baby to Operation Viking Hammer

Once we arrived at the PUK headquarters in Halabja, I looked around to find the rest of my team. The Headquarters building had been damaged by so much sporadic mortar and rocket fire from AAI over the years that I think they gave up trying to keep windows in it. I quickly found my team in a small grey room, very plain, no windows, with a poured concrete floor. I settled in.

We spent the next day planning with C Company, who was in charge of the attack. My team was the only team from B Company in Halabja, because we were familiar with the area and had deep rapport with the Kurdish leadership due to repetitive exposure to the situation and people during AFO. The general plan was to perform tactical preparations and recons for a few days, then we would mount the assault when my leadership felt like we had sufficiently planned and had some dedicated airpower. The Peshmerga leadership thought we should attack immediately, because we were just giving AAI too much time to prepare for our attack, and an opportunity for key people to escape. The Kurds reluctantly agreed to wait, although waiting was certainly not their style. We were also waiting to find out when the "Shock and Awe" barrage was going to happen. During the AFO mission we registered almost 70 targets against AAI, as well as hundreds of others along the Green Line, and we were wondering when that payload would arrive. Most of this planning took place between the C company commander, my Battalion commander, and each team's leadership. They decided who would comprise the "Attack Prongs." I thought the officers in charge of this operation were brilliant; they always accounted for things that I never thought of.

Finally, it was Shock and Awe night, which signaled the official start of the Iraq war in 2003. On that night, I stood on the roof of the Kurdish headquarters, with a very clear view of AAI's giant mountain den. The crooked outline of AAI's mountains along the Iranian border was so black it was barely discernable from the night sky. I stood next to my battalion commander, Ltc Tovo.

All the people on the roof became silent when an ominous buzzing sound materialized from the distant sky behind us. The noise then changed from a buzz to a low hum, like the sound of a very small and slow aircraft, and it was, in slow gradations, increasing in volume and decreasing in range. In only a few seconds, the sounds multiplied, then became omnipresent and louder, and I deduced that they were coming from multiple directions. The eerie sounds grew and surrounded us until I felt like I was standing within some kind of robotic, relentless swarm of bees that were invisible in the night sky as they streamed overhead towards AAI's mountains. I watched AAI's tracers fly straight up in the air and listened to automatic weapons fire as AAI and IGK positions started firing wildly into the sky at the sounds. A Kurdish man behind me giggled at their pathetic attempt to stop the 70 Tomahawk missiles that mindlessly approached their mountain fortress.

The black mountainside was suddenly saturated with explosions of fire in rapid succession; it was really an immeasurable and unexplainable level of violence. The explosions looked like the surface of boiling water when it reaches a "rolling boil," except instead of rolling froth on the surface, this was continuous orange and red flames against an enormous blanket of darkness. I thought I was going to count the explosions, but once the Tomahawks started hitting, there was no way to count them; it was the most relentless and devastating thing I had ever seen in my life. There were at least thirty or forty that all hit within less than a minute; the concussion from each strike became a part of the air I breathed, and I felt the bass of each explosion in my gut. Straggler missiles continued to buzz over our heads for the next hour or so and wreaked further havoc. Not only had AAI been bombed, but the IGK positions we registered were also hit.

The next day, the Kurdish PUK commander was not entirely convinced that the tomahawk strikes had been as effective as they were sensational. He thought the AAI fighters probably heard the missiles approaching and had time to get away from anywhere that would have been obviously targeted. However, he did agree that we may have taken out a few of their heavy weapons, such as mortars, and possibly some landmines, which was a positive. We killed over 100 IGK members at their headquarters near Khurmal – the result of passing through their lines to target AAI during AFO.

We continued preparation for Operation Viking Hammer; planning, mortar attacks, and reconnaissance were the duties for the next couple days.

I and a few other "mortar men" (The 18B MOS is highly proficient in mortars) from C company loaded our 81mm mortars into a truck along with a few dozen rounds of ammo, and as many Kurds as we could fit. We drove southeast towards the AAI enclave outside of Biyara to a planned location where we could strike some of the AAI positions with the mortars. We drove until we found a good spot behind the crest of a hill and sent spotters up to the top of the ridge to find some AAI positions. I was a spotter.

As I stayed low on the ridge, I peered across the expansive layers of massive ridgelines, and I noticed that AAI was very well dug into the mountains. They had established many positions in depth. AAI were not amateurs; they had controlled their 300 square kilometer mountain area for more than two years, and they were prepared to defend it.

Soon we had established a target, a big concreate bunker that was probably 20 X 20 feet, and we spotted some actual AAI fighters meandering around it. I watched their bearded forms through a spotting scope, and I guessed that they were licking their wounds from the tomahawk barrage; I saw them talking and I could read their expressions. It was alarming to look at other human beings through the mortar site, thinking that I was about to start killing them, but I recognized that any one of them would have chopped my head off if they could. Since we didn't see any mortars on their side anywhere close, we decided to bring the mortars up to the top of the ridge so we could use a technique called "direct lay," which is much faster and less technical way to fire mortars. We quickly analyzed the AAI bunker; it had thick overhead cover. This meant that if a mortar exploded on top, it might shake them up a bit, but probably wouldn't kill them. So, we had to get creative.

We developed a plan to drop "sub-surface burst" rounds onto the top of the positions, immediately followed by a volley of "near-surface burst" rounds. Sub-surface burst rounds do not explode when they hit the ground, they explode on a time delay *after* they hit the ground. This means the weight of the plummeting round will drive it into the overhead cover before it explodes, thus penetrating their overhead protection before exploding. This would cause the AAI guys to either die in place or run out of the bunker into the open. The near surface burst rounds explode about 4 meters off the ground and are designed to spray shrapnel downward in a cone, which is very effective against "troops in the open." Our idea was that the sub-surface barrage would force them to evacuate the bunker only to find themselves in a hail of explosions and shrapnel from rounds exploding over their heads. It was ingenious, albeit quite brutal.

I was a gunner on one of the 81MM tubes. By "gunner" I mean I was working the sight, levels, and "dialing in" the mortar instruments to get the rounds, and keep the rounds, on target (mortars are mechanically sophisticated). We gave the Kurds a quick class on how to safely drop the mortars down the tube, most of them knew how already, and soon I had a young, very excited Kurd ready to drop the first one. I lined up the mortar system perfectly with the target, but I knew that the first couple rounds would settle the baseplate and would significantly move the mortar, so I had to be quick about getting realigned, especially since I expected AAI to return fire.

I told the first Kurd to drop the round, and he did. The tube made a loud "poomf" sound, the baseplate sank into the ground, and I quickly realigned the mortar site and waited for impact. The round landed very close, so I quickly realigned, and told the next guy to drop the subsequent rounds. I was on target within three rounds and the baseplate was decently settled. I then instructed the Kurds to line up and administer the sequenced barrage.

The Kurds all stared at me with eager expressions on their faces; probably fifteen of them. They looked like a line in a department store, but instead of holding merchandise while waiting to pay, they were holding mortar rounds in the middle of the mountains, and I was the cashier. They walked up and dropped their rounds one by one the way we showed them. I realigned between each round until all the rounds were sent. The first round hit before the line finished. I watched through the mortar site, and the others watched through spotting scopes, as the mortars started to hit in rapid succession; I saw our plan come to life.

Several mortars landed near or on top of the large position (mortars are not pinpoint accurate). Through the dust I saw the AAI fighters try desperately to scramble out of the damaged position, some moved as if they were wounded already. When they reached a few feet away from the cover of the bunker, they were engulfed in overhead explosions. One of them was directly under a near surface burst blast. I saw his body contort, and then crumble lifelessly to the ground into an unnatural shredded heap through the lens of my mortar site.

As I expected, we started receiving AAI mortar fire, and although this was super scary initially, their fire was wildly inaccurate. Their rounds landed several hundred meters to my southeast, and subsequent rounds were all over the place; very inconsistent. The Kurds said the AAI mortars probably have no sights (which they claimed was quite common because it's hard to find working sights on the black market). During the day, we fired dozens of 81 MM mortars, and killed several AAI fighters, wounded others, and damaged a few fortified positions. We picked everything up and headed back to Halabja. From this day on we referred to what happened as "dueling mortars day."

The next day it was my team's turn to conduct reconnaissance operations, which meant we were going to penetrate AAI's territory. One of the guys on my team was an expert with the Barrett .50 Cal sniper rifle (a very large semi-automatic sniper rifle capable of killing at ranges over a mile away). Our plan was to penetrate about two kilometers into AAI territory, set up a position with the Barrett from which we had about a 1000 meter shot at a major AAI position on a hilltop that we referred to as "the pillbox." We thought we may be able to spot some AAI leadership and take them out.

We drove the vehicle slowly down the road, under cover, masked by terrain, until we reached a stopping point on the road about 1500 meters inside AAI's territory. An eerie, primal feeling came over me when we penetrated their territory. The Barrett gunner and I got out and walked across the road and down the steep embankment so we would be partially hidden from view. The terrain had no trees at all, and the ground was littered with fragments of flat stones and patches of grass. I felt overconfident that day, maybe all the air power and mortaring had given me a bit of a superiority complex.

As my gunner, the 18C (MOS for the Special Forces Engineer Sergeant) on my team, got situated behind the Barrett rifle, and I scanned the pillbox with the scope on my M21, suddenly a massive burst of machine gun fire snapped over my head and made powder out of some of the stones around me. The other guys were also taking fire over by the vehicle, and they jumped down behind a small roll of earth on the side of the dirt road.

My heart rate was instantly pegged as my gunner and I slid down just under the crest of the hill to get behind cover. I deduced that the rounds were coming from several heavy machinegun positions. I heard a flurry of noise from the direction of the pillbox that loosely correlated to the snapping sounds above my head. The guys on the road nominated one person to run to the truck to get ready to drive. Through the dust and noise, I watched them all dash for the vehicle. There was no way my gunner and I would have made it that far to the truck because the machine gun fire was all over the road above us. Using my radio, I told our Captain we would take the gully behind me back to the west, and then we would break north and link up with them back where we had some cover.

Just as I started hustling down into the valley behind us, thinking I was safe, I heard a horrible tearing sound in the huge sky above. I realized in an instant that it was the sound of an incoming mortar round. I'd heard mortars before, but this one seemed different. The sound got closer and closer, and I knew it was big and it was going to land close to us; my body tightened as if I had turned to stone with fear.

The 120-millimeter mortar slammed into the ground with unimaginable force and detonated no more than 40 meters away from us. I was facing it and saw it explode clearly; it sprayed dirt and rocks up and outwards like when a drop of liquid hits the surface of water, but with spectacular rapidity and violent energy. The concussion from the detonation rippled through my body and dropped me to my knees while my ears and head rang like a bell. Although my ears rang intensely, I still heard shrapnel and dirt and stone zinging through the dusty air as bullets continued to snap overhead. I yelled to my gunner to see if he was OK as I patted myself frantically looking for indications of shrapnel wounds; neither one of us was hit.

The round had landed just on the other side of a sizable piece of exposed ledge, and that sliver of ledge was between us and the explosion, so I think it deflected the shrapnel away from us. It was pure luck we were not killed or mutilated. We brushed ourselves off and continued to run lower into the gully. I tried to radio to my Captain, but we had lost radio communications with him. We continued to follow the ravine, and soon I was not exactly sure where we were. I thought AAI would dispatch a small contingent of fighters to track us down, but they either didn't, or we evaded them successfully.

I was thankful when I heard the Peshmerga firing mortars to suppress the AAI positions, and some of our guys also fired the MK19 machine gun at their positions. After about 20 lonely minutes in the bottom of a massive valley floor, we were back inside friendly lines, and we linked up with the rest of the team. Our sniper/recon mission turned out to be totally pointless and it had almost cost us our lives. I learned to never get complacent again.

We made our way back to the Halabja headquarters. I felt humbled, shaken up, and downright lucky. I cleaned my rifle, hung out with the Kurds and had some tea, and we told our war story to everyone, much to their entertainment. The Kurds told us we were lucky that AAI didn't capture and publicly behead us.

The next day I stood among all of C Company, watching our leadership and the Peshmerga leaders walk everyone through the final attack plan for Operation Viking Hammer. I could tell that the Kurdish leaders were not enthused about the depth of planning detail we had forced them to think through and explain.

The C Company B-Team had built a gigantic terrain model of the entire AAI enclave. The model was built "to scale" out of dirt, and it was probably 40 feet by 40 feet square. Terrain models are fundamental in military planning, and this was the mother of all terrain models that I had ever seen. The Kurdish leaders, and the leader of each prong, used long sticks as pointers to walk through their piece of the plan. I was proud of the way my captain talked through our piece. The plan, in summary, was quite simple from our perspective. Most of my team was the "main effort" of the attack, and we were called the *yellow prong*. Our responsibility was to secure the chemical facility in Sargat and clear the small village further east called Daramar. The Green prong consisted of the other half of my team and several personnel from C Company, and their mission was to cover our advances up the Sargat valley by clearing the ridge to our north. There were orange and red prongs as well, and they were responsible for zones south of us.

The leader of each prong finished briefing their plans. The PUK leadership and my officers declared that we were ready to go. I was told my battalion commander and Uncle Andy spoke to Donald Rumsfeld on the phone, and he said it was time to go for it.

The preparations were over. Now it was time to fight.

# Chapter 7
## Sargat Valley, Northern Iraq, 2003
## Operation Viking Hammer

*Location of Operation Viking Hammer. (Map source: OpenStreetMap)*

I laid on the concrete floor on a short piece of foam padding, trying to keep warm. I listened to everyone on my Green Beret team nervously tossing and turning in the pitch blackness of our grey concrete room at the PUK headquarters in Halabja. My M21 sniper rifle was perched on its bipod next to me; it was the tool that I would carry into battle against a thousand AAI extremists in the morning. I had my hand on its buttstock most of the night, thinking about how after 12 years of service, my big day had finally come. During the night, I left the room and unloaded all my magazines, 20 of them, to make sure the springs were properly stretched so I wouldn't have a feed malfunction during the battle. I actually went through this ritual twice, because I thought I had forgotten to check one of the magazines the first time. I heard my captain leave the room once with all of his combat gear, probably to do some similar preparations.

Finally, at about 4 AM, after a mostly sleepless night, one of our most familiar Peshmerga leaders came in and told us that it was time to go. I ate breakfast silently standing around a rustic table with about a dozen of the Kurdish PUK Peshmerga leaders in a dimly lit room. It was fried eggs and rice. I scanned the faces of the warriors standing around the table in full Peshmerga garb, some of our eyes met and we exchanged subtle head nods. Everyone's facial expressions were earnest to the extreme.

After breakfast, I put on my kit. I made sure my vest was tight, grenades were secure, pistol was holstered with a round chambered, medical kit was in place, camelback was full, and I double checked that my radio was charged. I picked up my M21 rifle, which my team referred to as "Old Sarge." I gripped it with confidence and familiarity, made sure the scope was set to 500 meters, and that the scope caps were tight. I pulled the bolt back just enough to see a glimmer of shiny brass to ensure a round was chambered, and I made sure Old Sarge was on safe. My "kit" and weapon were a physical extension of my body and mind; I was a machine in this regard.

In accordance with the battle plan, my team had organized into four separate elements. Three of my teammates, one carrying a Barrett .50 caliber sniper rifle, were part of the Green Prong. The other part of my team organized into another three smaller groups and we constituted the Yellow Prong. I was the leader of one group of the three yellow prong elements, and my objective was to stay on the front line of the attack into Sargat. My Team Sergeant and one of my other teammates formed another Yellow Prong element, and their mission was also to push the front line with a different group of Kurds. My Captain, Uncle Andy, and some other CIA personnel constituted the command-and-control element. Each of our teams was going to integrate into a 500 to a 1000 strong Peshmerga force.

The mission of the yellow prong, and the purpose of Operation Viking Hammer, was to secure the Sargat Chemical Facility: a place that had gained national level interest because of its potential to tie Sadaam to Al Qaida, and because it was suspected to contain evidence of chemical weapons or poisons production. I couldn't believe I was finally part of something this big.

I walked outside and glanced into the dark sky, then walked to the trucks through a crowd of hundreds of Kurds that were shining flashlights onto the tan colored dirt and concrete buildings inside the compound, chattering with one another in Kurdish as they prepared weapons and ammunition. We loaded our .50 caliber and MK19 along with tripods and ammo cans into the back of a small white pickup truck. I boarded the back of another similar pickup truck that had small benches in the bed. I sat down, and placed Old Sarge's buttstock on the floor, barrel up, and squeezed it tightly with my famous black leather fingerless gloves that now had duct tape keeping the cutoff fingers from falling apart; the same gloves I was wearing that memorable day in Kosovo. I reflected on that experience for a second until the Kurdish driver started the truck and took off in the general direction of AAI's lair in the massive mountains that loomed a short distance away. Along the bumpy road, I watched the outline of the dark, jagged mountains grow crisper against the sky as the sun rose behind them. My senses started to tingle as my nervousness increased.

As the truck grew closer to the small village of Dekon, and the sun had risen a bit more, a bewildering scene materialized before me as I squinted and peered into the distance through the dust from over the roof of the moving truck. I saw thousands of Peshmerga everywhere. A giant dark and tan blob of them sprawled for a mile wide across the sparsely grassed flatlands on the foothills of the snowcapped mountains that marked the Iranian border. The massive expanse of the Peshmerga horde was interspersed with hundreds of cars and trucks and other vehicles of all types, coming and going from as far as I could see in every direction. The cool breeze pushed the rising dust up and away, thousands of feet into the huge, orange, dawn sky above the sprawl of warriors. Belts of machine gun bullets and worn weapon's barrels reflected in the burgeoning sun and twinkled like space matter from within the giant cluster of Kurdish warriors. The sheer scale of this operation was astounding.

As the truck grew closer, I was able to distinguish Peshmerga fighters of all ages pouring out of taxi cabs, overloaded small cars, pickup trucks, farming tractors, motorcycles, and all of them were wearing their best PUK Peshmerga attire. Some had pistols with fancy handles stuffed into their waistbands, most had AKs, but some had belt-fed machine guns, shotguns, or hunting rifles. Some had colorful bags or backpacks with embroidered flowers and other designs on them, and still others had brought the whole family along.

As I scanned the crowd of black and white checkered head wraps, baggy brown pants, and moustaches, I was confused by the presence of a few extra-large heavy construction style dump trucks. After I watched Peshmerga cram into the back of them, I realized that these dump trucks were actually Peshmerga *armored personnel carriers*. I also took special notice of a fascinating green flatbed truck, very large, about the size of a 2.5-ton Army truck. This truck had a giant two barreled anti-aircraft machine gun bolted to its bed, and it reminded me of a battleship. I also spotted many land rovers that had 106 MM recoilless rifles or Katoosha rocket pods mounted to them.

As we approached and then penetrated the edge of the Kurdish mass, the collective murmur of thousands of Peshmerga became audible, grew louder and louder, and then the smell of human feces mixed with dust and body odor became overwhelming. The Kurds cheered vigorously for us alongside the truck as we parted the sea of them, with their weapons raised into the air above intense dark eyes. I waved and smiled to them as the truck became surrounded and slowly crept towards the center of the sprawling Peshmerga horde.

The Kurdish leadership expected between eight and ten thousand Kurds to show up. I estimated that the crowd of Peshmerga covered at least one entire square kilometer, not counting the vehicles everywhere on the fringes. This war against AAI was like a community event to the PUK, and Kurds from all over Northeastern Iraq had hitched a ride any way they could to get there.

We got off the truck and found the Kurdish leaders that we would fight alongside. We also conversed randomly amongst ourselves to help cope with our nervousness. It wasn't long before the nervousness got the best of me, and I really needed to use a bathroom. Someone told me there was a small shed about 250 meters away through the crowd that was "the bathroom." I navigated through the crowd for a few minutes, and hundreds of smiling Kurds patted my back and admired the scope on my weapon. One Kurd said, "I love your George Bush!" emphatically only inches from my face. Finally, I cut through the gracious and smelly crowd and made it to the shed.

When I opened the clumsy wooden door, I instantly knew the shed was the source of the intense fecal smell. There were two mountains of shit in the two back corners of the shed, and the holes in the floor were not even visible anymore. There was a metal rake leaned against the wall so people could make space to defecate by raking other people's shit to the corners. There were smear marks on the walls where the Kurds had wiped off their left hands. I used the rake to clear a spot and there was fecal matter on the handle, and I got some on my black leather gloves. I did my business and left as fast as I could; it was unbelievable, but I had bigger things to worry about.

It was full daylight when I walked out into the fresher air, and I reached down and grabbed some sand to clean my gloves. I instantly noticed that all the Kurds in my immediate vicinity were very intensely facing the mountains, and some murmured to each other in low serious voices without looking at each other. I curiously faced the mountains as well, to see what they were all looking at. I saw the dark silhouettes of AAI fighters along the first ridgeline watching us with defiance, and I instantly knew why everyone looked so solemn. The scene reminded me of the movie Braveheart, where the two enemies faced off before battle, and like the movie, we were just waiting for a signal to begin the charge.

I made my way back through the crowd to where my team was, and my Captain told me there were aircraft inbound to "prep" the front ridgeline ("prep" is a fancy military term for bombing the hell out of somewhere before you go in). As the sound of the approaching aircraft became audible in the distance, I watched the AAI fighters run back off the ridge out of my view, just before the ridgeline burst into violent explosions as three or four large bombs dropped in succession along the crest. The boom of the thunderous explosions shook the earth and sent a tingling shock through my body, and the crowd of Peshmerga cheered vigorously, at least until the AAI fighters reappeared on the ridge not more than a minute later.

At that moment, a fear arose that I had never felt before. The feeling was the uniquely primitive brand of fear that settles in when a person realizes that another group of human beings wants to kill them.

A Peshmerga man in his 40s, who had his weapon slung and wore a typical pair of tan baggy Peshmerga pants climbed up the side of the battleship truck, which was now completely encircled by hundreds of restless Peshmerga. He expertly manipulated the creaky cranks and wheels until the massive cannon pointed in the direction of the AAI figures on the ridge. The barrels of the weapon were probably ten feet long, and they both had large cylinders on the ends that looked like giant silencers.

The Kurd fired the weapon, and my ears instantly rang from the noise. The cannon made an exceptionally loud disturbing metal-on-metal grating sound when it fired. The sharp repetitive bark of the weapon rolled like thunder towards the mountains, and then echoed back with diffusion. The unnatural smell of gunpowder from the cannon mingled with the smell of shit and body odor, and then drifted over the murmuring horde in the cool breeze. The battleship's tracers looked like glowing weightless softballs as they flew towards the ridge. I assumed the battleship was firing flak rounds because the rounds exploded in the air above the ridge. The cannon fired so fast and powerfully, and it rocked the truck back and forth so violently, that the surrounding Peshmerga horde rippled as hundreds of men recoiled from around it. The battleship made the AAI Fighters scramble, and again dozens of their dark forms disappeared over the ridge.

The firing of the battleship was the signal to charge. The Peshmerga mob stirred, and their chatter grew louder as my heartrate surged in anticipation. The handful of Green Berets, CIA, and Air Force Operators, dispersed among the unorganized line of trucks and the crowd of rag-bag Kurdish warriors began to ooze towards the mountains, compelled by an unspoken force of energy and unity. As I advanced among a sea of fighters, a low and gruff war cry began to emulate from the masses. It was like how the men in Braveheart yelled as they began to charge the enemy, except we were all carrying rifles and machine guns instead of broad swords and battle axes.

I jumped into the back of a light pickup truck as it crept towards the enemy. From my elevated position in the back of the pickup, I was floating on top of an impetuous tan colored sea of weapon clad Peshmerga wearing black and white head wraps, all of whom were trotting, elbow to elbow, eyes trained on AAI's mountain stronghold. Some AAI fighters were running along the ridge. Soon there were more Kurds firing the 106s, and the battleship continued to fire over our heads onto the ridge to help secure our approach to the valley entrance.

We reached a destroyed AAI checkpoint and the Green Prong branched off, as planned, and they hustled towards the ridgeline to my left. I wished them well, and I watched my teammates walk straight up the enormous ridge distributed among their Peshmerga until they became indistinguishable shapes among their horde. I continued forward towards the opening of the valley, and then I heard the Green Prong come under fire, which made the hair stand up on the back of my neck because I knew it wouldn't be long until we made contact as well.

We continued towards the mouth of the Sargat valley and drove by one of the checkpoints that we had observed so many times during Advanced Force Operations. There was a burnt and now rotting lower leg laying on the ground with the jagged tibia completely exposed. The foot was still wearing a boot, and there was shredded skin, meat, and shards of clothing attached. The Kurds kicked the rotting human leg out of the way emotionlessly as we all continued to move forward another couple hundred meters. There were around 1500 Kurds spread out behind and in front of me when we finally stopped. I dismounted and glanced in the direction of the sound of the Green Prong's sporadic firing.

I moved rapidly on foot along the windy dirt road, a mere speck within the enormity of the Peshmerga crowd, careful not to venture into the long grass because the Kurds had told us prior that there were landmines, which made me perceive the grass as frightening and unnatural. As I walked up the valley among the mass of Peshmerga towards the enemy my sense of imminent danger increased with each step.

I continued around the bend and finally the great expanse of the Sargat valley extended before me. To my left I saw a blur of rough green and brown grass extending for thousands of yards along a massive bald ridge with jagged rocks strewn all over the place. The bombs that were dropped a few minutes prior had perverted the landscape, had thrown blackened rocks everywhere, and sent a burnt ozone smell into the air. To my front, the narrow, light-brown, dirt road slithered up the sparsely grassy and rocky valley floor up and through a small village called Gulp, which was about one kilometer away. The village had jagged but beautiful layers of snowcapped mountains far behind its primitive outline. These mountains marked the Iranian border, and essentially comprised the finish line for this attack, which looked like a hundred miles away. To my right I observed a small knoll with a few small shrub-like trees on top and some piles of rocks. I was glad that I brought Old Sarge and not my M4 carbine as I gazed across the expansive terrain – 7.62/308 caliber just had better ballistics for this type of environment.

I made radio contact with my company mortar team as I continuously scanned the hills to my front along with the horde that surrounded me. I was encircled by a whirling blur of tan MC Hammer pants, thick black moustaches, white and black head wraps, the yellow glistening of belts of machine gun bullets, the rattle of weapons, the smell of body odor, and incessant nervous chatter in Kurdish. My senses were overloaded by the size of the terrain, the crowd of smelly warriors chattering and clattering around me, and the sound of pitched shouting and machine gun fire from the Green prong to my left. So far, this attack was everything I had dreamed it would be.

Suddenly, AAI machine gun fire erupted from my right and front simultaneously. It was like the world around me instantly froze, and then became a mirror that shattered into fractals of confusion and sunlight and sky and blue and green as

I searched for cover. The Peshmerga began sprinting toward the sound of machine gun fire, and their murmuring turned into frantic shouting as bullets snapped overhead and weapons fire echoed around me. My heart rate and nerves surged. There was nowhere to take cover. I was on an open road in an open valley, with possible landmines off the road. That feeling of nakedness and doom that I had felt a few days prior when that mortar almost hit me swept over me again.

I jumped down into the prone position in a small rut on the side of the road, a pathetic attempt at cover, relieved that I hadn't exploded due to a landmine, and began to scan the knoll to the right through my rifle's scope to try and identify where the fire was coming from. I could see the Peshmerga on the offensive, already at the bottom of the knoll, running in a swarm towards the firing. I spotted what looked like an AAI Fighter near a pile of rocks, but I could not confirm well enough that it was not a Kurd. The Peshmerga were moving so fast that they could have made it there by then, so I didn't take the shot.

Bullets were flying everywhere. Tracers bounced off the hillsides and dirt around me. The Kurds continued to spread out in flanking operations, having no choice but to accept the risk of landmines and venture off the road.

I began to run towards Gulp with my three-man team to the front line of our Kurds, but slowed down, looked up, and scanned the sky when I heard the rapidly growing sound of a Jet flying at low altitude, approaching from behind us. All the Peshmerga around me intensely scanned the sky with both fear and awe in their concentrated eyes, mouths agape under dark moustaches. As the aircraft grew rapidly closer, it sounded like a knife was ripping through the atmosphere like it was a giant piece of heavy blue canvas. The ear-piercing sound of the jet grew even more colossal and unnatural when the pilot fired a massive burst from the aircraft's main machine gun at the hillside just beyond Gulp. The hillside burst into dust as if it had erupted instantly, and I felt each of the hundreds of small explosions in my gut. I instinctually crouched in response to the devastation I had just witnessed as I ran towards Gulp. The AAI fire stopped, and the Kurds and I cheered triumphantly; The motivational effect of the airstrike was instantly realized. The Peshmerga horde, and I among them, sprinted and screamed towards Gulp as the noise of the aircraft faded and became a background tone for the Kurdish chatter and battle rattle that surrounded me.

The magnitude of the scene was almost imperceptible as I ran along the road. Thousands of Kurdish fighters ran and yelled towards the hills, the sound of machine gun fire was omnipresent, aircraft streaked overhead, the smell of burnt ground and body odor mixed with machine gun grease flooded my flared nostrils, wounded Peshmerga limped past me, and the Kurds were thoroughly distributed across the vast terrain like locusts.

It's difficult to convey in writing how when one suddenly faces death, how refined and primitive one's thinking becomes. Survival instinct must be at the core of how I became like an animal, keen in my senses, sagacious in my movements, head clear of all worldly distractions. I realized later, this primordial clearing of one's head to focus on survival for prolonged periods of time is what makes it hard to psychologically recover from war; to readapt to a world where other-than-survival actually matters.

When I think about that movement into Gulp, I often reflect on the way the Peshmerga operated. They flowed through mountains like a large adaptive and self-organizing horde. When any piece of the horde is engaged, a contingent of appropriate size ("appropriate" is determined instantly based on instinct) is dispatched to eliminate that threat. A new element of the horde then takes to the front, and the horde continues to move forward, never stopping, never pausing, ever. Most of the elements within the horde were likely based on hometown, tribe, or even possibly by family. Radios were in short supply, so separation into many smaller groups would have made communication impossible. When the Peshmerga were in battle, they reminded me of life forms that have swarm intelligence, like bees, ants, or when starlings swarm in the sky. They move like a single adaptive organism, and don't need much more than a general direction and a desired end-state to make things happen. There was beauty in their method; fast, agile, simple, and brutally effective. It was really pointless that any of us even carried guns when we were integrated with the Peshmerga. In fact, now I think it was pointless that the US ever deployed conventional troops to Iraq at all, given that the Green Berets of the 10th Special Forces Group (and some from 3rd Group and AFSOC) had collectively organized over one hundred thousand Kurds who would have gone anywhere with us. I wonder what would have happened in Iraq if we'd taken a purely Unconventional, Surrogate warfare approach? I digress.

We made it to Gulp, and I stopped and stood next to a very old stone Mosque; the one I had seen from a distance. The Mosque had two holes in its roof, and I caught a glimpse of dead bodies on the inside through some openings in the primitive outer walls. In close vicinity to the Mosque, there were several dead AAI bodies on the ground. Blood trails from the bodies steamed in the cold morning air and ran like small rivers through the micro terrain near each corpse. I picked up one of the Radical Islamic teaching books that were scattered around the outside of the mosque. The cover had Arabic writing on it, and pictures of British and American flags burning with the Twin Towers smoking in the background.

The vehicles caught up with us, and we miraculously united with our truck that had our heavy weapons in the back, so I jumped into the back and we continued to advance towards Sargat. At Gulp, one large group of Peshmerga broke off and followed another Green Beret team (the Red prong) south, and another large horde continued with us. As we drove out of Gulp, I swallowed dust, inhaled the burnt air, and continued to look at the motionless dead bodies until they were masked by terrain.

We started receiving fire from a valley to our south and rounds pinged off the earth and stones around our truck. We all jumped out and I tried to locate the source of the fire, which I failed to do. I got frustrated because this was the second time we'd taken fire, and the second time I had been unsuccessful at identifying exactly where it was coming from. The terrain was incredibly huge and mostly light brown, with small tads of green, so the tan uniforms of the AAI fighters blended in well.

Combat is massively frustrating. It's not like the movies where people instantly identify who is shooting at them, and then they easily take them out. I couldn't see anything, and when the bullets are flying you can't just stand up and look around to find who's shooting at you. There is dust, sweat in your eyes, fog on your glasses, you're out of breath, the bad guys are moving, you're moving, and you have to stay behind cover. This moment outside Gulp is when I realized that this battle wasn't going to be as straight forward as my daydreams about war had been over the 12 years prior.

My Team Sergeant spotted them, and he told us to pull the MK19 off the truck and set it up. I faced up the hill to our east in case we were attacked from over the hill. He fired the MK19 for about 50 or so rounds and the AAI fire stopped. Either the AAI who were shooting at us died, or they ran away, or the advancing Kurds to our south took them out.

None of us knew that the Green and Red prongs (who were north and south of us respectively, as we all moved east) were flushing the bulk of the AAI fighters into Sargat. We were about to hit hundreds of them head on.

We quickly threw the MK19 in the truck, I jumped in the back again, and we kept moving forward. I could not see Sargat yet, but I knew it was right around the corner. Prior to the Attack during all the preparations, and because of all the intelligence we had collected on the AFO mission, my mind had constructed a vision of Sargat as some kind of evil medieval fortress or demonic monster, so my anxiety surged as I got closer. My small team and I dismounted and continued on foot among the Kurds.

In the distance across the valley, along the ridge, I saw the Green Prong's horde fighting their way forward along the high ground. I knew my teammates were amongst the mass of advancing human forms, and to myself I wished them luck. The gunfire, explosions, smoke, and Kurdish yelling increased in volume continuously as we progressed further east.

I rounded a corner caused by a spur in the terrain, and there were tracers flying and ricocheting everywhere. Dozens of Kurds screamed at us to get down with crazed intensity in their eyes and we ran for cover. One of my teammates had the M240 machine gun and a few Kurds helped us with ammo. We ran forward to where a cluster of Peshmerga was pinned down along the road, and I focused my vision intensely on the foot of the ridge on the other side of the valley where the majority of fire seemed to be coming from. The adrenaline was phenomenal.

We ran through a light sprinkling of snapping tracers until we found cover behind a very small finger that extended into the valley. The streaming tracer bullets that were accompanied by snapping sounds kept me low as we set up the M240 and I started spotting for AAI. There were a few AAI below a rocky part of the Green Prong's ridge about 300 meters away, firing up at the Green Prong as they advanced. All the Kurds around me fired into the same area, but their fire was not very effective. My teammate unleashed a hail of fire with the M240, and the AAI dispersed a bit while I scanned with Old Sarge.

Through my 10-power scope, I saw a bearded AAI fighter moving backwards, and firing upwards at members of the Green prong. I placed my mil dot crosshairs on his tan waist. At this range, since my scope was set to 500, I knew that aiming at his waist would put the round in the chest area. My training took over and I became super calm for a second, I completely ignored the chaos of war around me, and became hyper-aware of my own breathing.

I inhaled then slowly exhaled, and when my breath was almost all the way out, I carefully and smoothly squeezed the trigger. The rifle fired, and the round was on its way. Since I was in a steady position, my rifle's recoil did not kick enough to take my aim off the AAI fighter, and I watched him falter and fall to the ground, then crawl down the hill into some light trees or shrubbery. I fired a few more rounds in succession and he stopped moving.

The noise of war flooded back into my ringing ears and I realized that I lost sight of my Team Sergeant, as well as my Captain. I quickly assumed they were engaged somewhere else, so it was just my three-man team amongst a several hundred strong Peshmerga group. Our Kurds received a signal to move, likely by cell phone, or maybe pure instinct, so we started moving rapidly forward on the front line of the attack into Sargat.

My team and I jogged down the sparely grassed hill, off the road and onto the rocky and grassy valley floor along with our group of several hundred Kurds. Fifty or so Peshmerga were in my immediate vicinity, along with hundreds more slightly ahead and behind me in clear view. An old man of about 70 years old gave me a giant toothless grin and a big thumbs-up as he walked along with an AK in one hand and a cane in another.

As we continued incessantly forward, the tracer fire increased, and the mind shattering sound of combat grew towards a crescendo. The Green Prong was heavily engaged, and I heard the distinct bark of that Barrett .50 cal reverberate periodically. Mortars exploded, RPGs sizzled through the air, and tracers flew everywhere once I rounded the huge corner of the valley and cast my eyes upon the objective.

Sargat was a primitive, shamble of concrete dwellings sparsely interspersed with skinny wilted trees, eerily dark even under the clear midday sky. It looked like a giant bowl had been tilted towards me, with a rim made of massive olive and brown ridgelines. The back side of the bowl, which extended from beyond the main cluster of disorganized structures, was horizontally striped with enormous and twisted tendril-like lines of ledge. Nestled into the shadows of the tentacles were dozens of crooked grey concrete building structures, semi-organic to the ledges they were under, each with their own form, with black windowless openings that looked like empty black eyes. The tendrils looked like they were bleeding due to the erosion of reddish soil that was layered into the ledge outcroppings. The angle of the sun on the jagged ledges casted long lines of gloomy shadows down the steep hillsides. The occasional flashes of AAI weapon's fire from within the black eyes made them seem alive and mystical.

In the distance, birds flew fitfully from some of the sickly trees as explosions startled them, and they looked like mere specs in contrast to the scale of the terrain and geography around them. The rows of menacing white mountain peaks along the Iranian border loomed behind Sargat and projected a sense of governance over everything in the expanse below them. I felt impossibly small and insignificant as I jogged up the valley floor towards the sound of machine gun fire in a semi crouch as bullets snapped and whizzed by me.

The span of green valley that led into Sargat had staggered layers of stone walls running across it at random intervals. These stone walls were the only cover or concealment available except for a small ravine that was a thousand meters ahead of us. I didn't have time to perceive any more of the scene to fully orient myself, because I immediately began receiving an unimaginable volume of gun fire from our 10 and 12 o'clock. I sprinted through snapping tracers towards the protection of the nearest row of stone walls and dove down behind one. I still had no idea where my Team Sergeant and Captain were, which had me concerned, but I knew where my team was, and that we had a job to do: keep bounding forward with the front line and take the village.

As we fired and maneuvered from one stone wall to the next, one of the guys on my team fell and badly smashed his knee but kept going forward. With the amount of tracer fire, and other munitions exploding everywhere, it was nearly impossible to locate any AAI fighters to fire at. There were Kurds everywhere firing alongside us, and I was almost killed by a Kurdish machine gunner when I moved laterally to get to another stone wall; he smiled and nodded to me apologetically even though we both knew it was my fault. Mortars landed violently with intense concussion, earth upheaved, RPGs streamed through the air, and the three of us finished another sprint and made it to another wall. We smiled at each other and exchanged some comedic comments about what a nice day it was.

I attempted continuously to spot targets and fire at AAI from behind the wall. In one case, like a fool, I did not have my barrel above the stone wall, only my scope, and my round hit the wall right in front of my barrel when I fired. One of the guys on my team yelled "I saw that!" It was embarrassing, but I was too scared to care. The Kurds had staged the trucks along the road to our 4 o'clock, and one of the trucks had a 106MM recoilless rifle mounted on it.

The 106 had no sights on it, so to aim it, I watched the Peshmerga gunner open the breach, look through the barrel from back to front, and then move the gun until his target was in the center of the tube. He had so much experience with firing the weapon without real sights that he knew how to adjust for elevation based on his estimation of the distance. I heard him firing the cannon repeatedly over the other noise as we fought our way deeper into the valley toward Sargat, bounding from one row of stone walls to another under intense fire. My eyes darted from point to point with such rapidity that my senses couldn't process the changing images fast enough, and for a while it was as if I couldn't see anything at all.

My senses and fear were so inflated from the perpetual uncertainty of death, and primitive state of survival that swept over me, that my ability to smell became keen and animalistic. There was a heavy earthy and grassy smell in the air because of the dirt the mortar rounds were upheaving. The smell of the oil and carbon from my rifle, my black leather gloves, my breath, the smoke of munitions in the air, my sweat, and the crispness of the cool air were so strong I could taste them. The sounds were even more exaggerated than the smells. The rockets streaking, mortars tearing through the sky, the snap of bullets over my head, the bark of my own rifle, the deafening sound of the 106s, Kurdish machine gun fire, distressed Kurdish chatter, distant and near enemy machine gun fire which was correlated to the snapping sound over my head like the two were in harmony, and the ringing in my ears were all echoing back and forth in the valley and in my head, growing and growing with such intensity I thought the entire valley would detonate into oblivion.

I popped my head up to scan for AAI, and in slow motion, a tracer left the edge of one of the buildings on the outskirts of Sargat and whizzed just past the right side of my head with a snap. Every time I tried to locate any AAI from behind the wall in order to engage with my rifle, bullets streaked by my head and slammed into the wall in front of me with inconceivable force.

An unbounded and increasing stream of tracers poured over the stone wall, and bullets continued to slap into it. I looked down along the stone wall that extended to my left where my other two teammates were laying in the prone along with dozens of Peshmerga that had spread out between and beyond them. They popped up and down as they struggled to engage AAI, and tracers streamed past them all in depth.

We struggled like this for several hours; an eternity, trying with futility to locate and accurately fire back at AAI while taking heavy fire, until finally, as I scrambled around behind the walls, one of my teammates shouted to me, eyes full of bewilderment *"what the fuck are we going to do!?"* I tried to get a hold of the mortar team, but I could not reach them anymore. I tried to call my Captain, but I couldn't reach him either.

I had no idea what to do and I felt completely isolated; miniscule and helpless in the face of our situation. I thought to myself over and over.

*I am a Green Beret. I am supposed to know what to do.*

Within 30 seconds of primitive mental churn, options started to materialize in my sub-conscience while I tried to ignore the ambient sounds of war and the constant interruption of bullets ricocheting off the wall in front of me.

We could not move forward, because I didn't know where any of the AAI fighters really were. We'd have been shot instantly because of the sheer volume of fire and because there wasn't any more cover until we made it inside Sargat. Moving to the left made no sense, because there were no stonewalls there, and that meant no cover. There was no doubt that we had to move, and it appeared that to the right presented the highest probability of survival.

## One Green Beret

As my mind churned and I prepared myself to move, a new ominous sound joined the valley's war symphony. This sound was so deep and profound, it was like belt-fed thunder. This new sound originated from a very large heavy machine gun on the huge ridge to the east above Sargat, and it was mowing down the valley floor from an unknown AAI position.

The reality that the instrument which produced this new sound could at any nanosecond render me shredded to pieces on that valley floor, elicited an epic feeling of absolute and pervasive doom from within an unfamiliar and primitive place within my soul. I had never imagined such a feeling of oppression and imminent doom was possible. I was convinced that I was going to die, and I froze; I had no idea what to do.

Out of nowhere, through a horizontal rain of tracers, my Captain sprinted over to me from somewhere to my right and dove down beside me; his sudden presence confirmed my suspicion that we were in deep trouble. He asked me, yelling over the noise, if we were doing ok, and he told me there was cover to our right. As he sprinted away, half crouched, through a hail of bullets, I suddenly felt a rush of motivation; he inspired me. He had left his laminated and folded map on the ground next to me, and just as I picked it up, he came bouncing back over to get it. I said, "hey sir, I would have brought you your map, don't get yourself killed!"

My small team and I conversed briefly by shouting to each other over the incessant sounds and decided to move to the right or we were doomed. I also very suddenly decided that these terrorist nutjobs were not going to deprive me of seeing my newborn baby daughter and my wife again, and that was when the fear in my mind transformed to fury and hate, perhaps evil, like water suddenly reaching a rolling boil. I felt no emotion or sympathy for any life on earth other than my own and my team's. This rage was what I needed. So, with a newfound level of primal aggression, I told my team to start bounding to the right, and I prepared to move.

I got up and started running. I perceived an increase in the snapping sound of the bullets flying by me, the volume of my own heartbeat increased, and my own pulse rushed through my ears as I saw muzzle flashes out of the corners of both eyes. Everything was a blur, but within a few seconds, through the mist of my own kaleidoscopic perception, a small tunnel of clarity appeared ahead, and through this tunnel I saw a small gathering of people huddled behind a slightly higher portion of stone wall approximately 100 meters away. When I initially jumped up and ran, I had no idea where I was going, but now I had a specific destination.

After almost getting shot again by another Kurd who was behind a wall that I ran in front of, I dropped down behind another wall. When I got down AAI concentrated fire at the wall where they had seen me disappear, and I cursed out loud in response. I crawled about 20 feet, then popped up and made another final dash through the tracers until I reached the cluster of people behind the cover of the larger chunk of stone wall. I was relieved that I made it, and soon my other two teammates joined us.

My Captain, Uncle Andy, Bafel Talibani, and one of our interpreters were all there behind the wall. Bafel was talking to his father, Jalal Talibani (the future president of Iraq) on a satellite phone. His dad was mad at him for participating in the battle and putting himself in such danger. Uncle Andy, who probably read the shell-shocked look of fury on my face, told me this was the last time he would ever go on an operation with a bunch of crazy Green Berets; he was joking.

I spotted a few fleeting AAI Fighters about 250 meters away on the other side of a few buildings, and I shot at them, but I couldn't confirm whether it was my bullets that wounded them or someone else's. The ominous sound of the Heavy AAI machine gun continued as my Captain and Uncle Andy conversed by shouting in each other's ears over the noise.

They said we needed to get the .50 cal on to the high ground, to take out AAI's heavy machine gun.

My Captain told my team to make it happen.

The .50 cal was in the back of a pickup, and all the pickups were lined up 400 meters away to our 3 o'clock. I took a nervous deep breath, looked across the expanse of terrain and the density of tracers flying across it, then exhaled shakily. My whole body tightened as I peered across four football fields of streaming tracers that I was about to run through to get to those trucks.

All three of us simultaneously ran out into the pouring tracers; I felt like I broke the barrier to another dimension when I left the protection of the stone wall. As I ran, there were hundreds of Kurds firing past us and we continuously yelled to make sure they saw us coming so we didn't get shot by friendly fire. Heavy lines of tracers flew past me in both directions, like a laser light show, and bullets struck the ground and hills everywhere. I was so tense, braced in anticipation for the impact of a bullet, I felt as if my muscles might rip out of my skin. A large caliber tracer struck a washed-out embankment and ricocheted upwards, spinning very fast like some kind of firework. It arced over our heads and we ran under it like a ring of fire. We were in awesome physical condition, so the sprint didn't bother us, even though we were each carrying about 50 pounds of kit.

Finally, breathing heavily, but extremely focused and unimaginably furious, I reached the white Nissan truck. One of my teammates jumped in the driver's seat, I got into the passenger seat, and another jumped in the back. Just as I sat down and the vehicle lurched forward into the flurry of bullets, a bullet penetrated the front windshield with a pop and a zing and went out the open door next to me; it passed right in front of my face. My teammate floored it and we drove for about 300 meters until we turned up a very small trail and stopped. We dismounted.

There was a huge green hill to our front, which completely blocked my view of Sargat. On my left, I could still see the valley of Kurds being suppressed by a relentless volley of tracers. We needed to bring the .50 cal machine gun, and a sufficient amount of ammo, to the top of this hill. I smelled the earth and grass, and then the terrifying sound of AAI's heavy machine gun spoke again as I reached the bed of the truck to get the .50 cal. My teammate, our communications sergeant, a beast of a man, grabbed the 80 plus pound machine gun and easily hoisted it onto his shoulder, prepared to run up the hill with it. My other teammate grabbed the tripod for it, which was also at least 20 pounds. I slung Old Sarge and grabbed 2 ammo cans, and so did a half a dozen Peshmerga who showed up to help.

We sprinted up the massive ridge, 300 meters to get to the top along a 45 degree or steeper angle. We charged upwards like machines, like Olympians with guns, on a mission to dominate the valley and get out alive. I dug the toes of my boots so furiously into the grass and dirt as I powered up the hill that I could feel individual small pebbles through the soles, and I breathed mechanically with each stride.

I reached the crest of the hill and my thighs were pumped, and my heart was almost exploding in my chest. Miraculously, I spotted a divot in the ground on the top of the ridge. The ridge was completely bald, green, and rounded on the top, and this divot enabled us to set up the .50 cal and have a small amount of protection. I was able to see the entire expanse of Sargat. From on top of the ridge, my eyes rendered the dark scene below me like an abstract painting that was alive with violence.

We crawled up and got into the divot, which was only about a foot deep. I saw a Kurd get shredded by machine gun fire on the front side of the hill as his group tried to advance from the south; he was sickeningly dismantled as tracers passed through his body. I also identified the Sargat Chemical Facility compound for the first time; our objective. It was right below our position on the ridge. I recognized it because I had memorized the overhead imagery prior.

From up there on that ridge, the sound of war in the valley had a different feel to it, more ambient with more reverb, but louder, as if the valley was boiling over with noise, a cacophony of death. The sounds of war are unforgettable, especially the coalesced sound of screaming human voices, loaded with such an abnormally high amount of agony, fear, stress, and urgency. From the divot, I scanned the bowl and searched for the location of AAI's machine gun.

I quickly identified a dark grey concrete structure with a single black opening that lit up as large tracers flew from it. I knew It was where the heavy machine gun was by correlating the sound to the flashes amongst the other noise. My teammates had already set up the .50 cal on its tripod, and it was ready for action. I pointed out the building to my team, which was probably 600 meters away. My communications guy didn't hesitate and began firing the .50, which increased the noise in the valley tenfold. We immediately came under fire in response, and I slid down as low as I could into the divot. I laid my weapon on its side so I could stay low and still look through the scope sideways. My teammate walked his .50 cal tracers onto the flashing building, and I helped feed ammo from the different ammo cans. My fear was that we would not destroy their gun before AAI got on target with us; it was like a duel, so we had to be quick. Soon we were absolutely shredding the structure, and we just kept hammering it until we had fired about 600 rounds into it. As my teammate fired, I looked through my scope and saw our bullets actually passing *through* the structure. The AAI tracers stopped emitting, and the building stopped flashing.

They Kurds below us began to advance when we started firing. The Peshmerga stampede flooded the perimeter of the evil fortress of Sargat and swept through it like ants suddenly rushing through the paths of a large and complex ant farm. I glanced at the now dark and empty AAI machine gun structure one last time before we packed up the .50 cal and ran down off the hill rapidly. We went through the ruins of the chemical facility, careful not to touch the extremely hot barrel of the .50 cal. When we got to the bottom, and linked up with my Captain, the strangest thing happened.

## One Green Beret

The Kurds brought us assorted meats on what looked like a silver platter.

We ate our lunch quickly from behind a berm on the side of a road that had been carved out of the ridge, within a few feet from the poison and chemical facility, which looked like a pile of rubble with some remaining structure and a fence around it. A fairly consistent trickle of tracers still flew and snapped overhead. There was still fighting going on, but it appeared that the bulk of the work to take Sargat was over and the Kurds had it covered. While we ate, several truckloads of wounded and dead Kurds that were being moved back to Halabja drove by. One such truck, which in its bed carried a pile of about 10 Kurd's bodies, stopped next to us and our medic examined a disfigured man who had been shot in the leg, face, and shoulder. As they drove away, human blood ran from the bed of the truck like a thick crimson waterfall, and my stomach knotted at the sight of so much blood.

We finished eating quickly, thanked the Kurds, and began to drive around the south side of Sargat, past and away from the chemical facility. We drove around the southern perimeter of Sargat to a very rough road that climbed the steep terrain along switchbacks very near to where that heavy machine gun was. As I looked down the hill across the expanse of Sargat, I was stunned by the sheer volume of dead bodies everywhere. There was a body every 10 or 15 feet, motionless in unnatural positions for almost as far as I could see. The sound of war echoed from a riverbed to my left as we climbed the rough mountain switchbacks.

We finally reached a plateau, and I saw a few buildings in the distance from the back of the truck. We had two or three land rovers and trucks, one of them had a 106MM recoilless rifle mounted on it. As we got closer, we stopped the vehicles on the outer edge of a cluster of dilapidated concrete buildings, dismounted, and continued on foot to clear this relatively small area. This was Daramar.

As we approached the shoddy buildings, I realized how high we had climbed into the mountains, and how massive the white snowcapped peaks were along the Iranian border. There were no AAI fighters in the buildings, so we moved some of the vehicles closer. We had 15 or so people with us; Uncle Andy, Bafel Talibani, my team, an interpreter, and a group of Peshmerga surrounded me.

As we reached the easternmost building, just as we thought everything was clear, we started receiving withering machine gun fire from a ridge directly in front of us. We all jumped down behind a building, which the AAI machine guns incessantly chipped away at, and I was again astonished and terrified by the sheer force of the bullets' impact.

That same black wave of doom and helplessness swept over me again when I realized that this battle wasn't over, and we were in big trouble again.

Bullets slapped and ricocheted off the building at an alarming rate. Rounds struck the ground and streamed by each side of the building. I was concerned that there might be another group of AAI advancing on us under the cover of the machine gun fire. We couldn't just sit there and allow ourselves to get surprised, and the Kurds knew this. They started running over to the 106 truck to return fire. I moved to the left side of the building, laid as flat as I could to minimize exposure, and looked through my scope to see if I could identify the source of the fire. Nothing but rocks became apparent to me, and again I was brutally irritated that the firing was too intense for me to get a decent look at anything. It was like fighting against ghosts.

My team sergeant and my medic crawled up next to me, and they put the .50 cal into operation. The machine gun fire came from a ridge that ran perpendicular to the way we were facing, and I saw a few AAI fighters dashing around the rocks on the ridge to our front. I fired at them as my teammates got the .50 set up. I could not tell if I hit anything, but I just continued to lay down fire because I thought it might cause some of them to move, and then we'd at least be able to locate them.

Grit fired the .50, and as soon as he did, the AAI machine gun fire increased. I ran backwards to a position behind the 106 truck, where I huddled tightly next to Bafel against the tailgate, where we both crouched helplessly as bullets pinged off the truck almost musically and kicked up dirt all around us. I looked down and to my right as I crouched, and saw bullets hitting the soft dirt just a few inches away from my foot; I was terrified as I imagined those bullets tearing through my soft flesh and bone if they shifted over just a few inches. A Kurd ran over and loaded the 106 and prepared to fire. Based on the way he was talking and pointing I assumed he had identified a target. The 106's breach was right above my head; I was crouched under it. The concussion alone from a 106 can be dangerous, and I braced myself as the Kurd slammed a shell into the breach, closed it, and prepared to fire; he was fearless.

The Kurd fired the 106 and the blast wave rippled through my entire body and my brain jiggled in my skull. I had fired a 106 before many times so at least I wasn't surprised by the force of the blast. We were in this situation for several minutes, the gunner continuously fired the 106 from over my head, and the ringing in my ears and pain in my body grew with each blast. My teammates had abandoned the .50, and I was not sure where they were. After a few more 106 rounds, I was almost completely deafened, my whole body ached, and I ran back behind one of the buildings through a stream of tracers.

As we sprinted back to take cover, my Captain told us that an aircraft was inbound to provide air support. My medic, who we called "Hap," severely burned his hand on the .50 cal barrel as we dashed backwards. As I ran back to take new cover, rounds struck the ground just in front of me, and also splashed up dirt just behind Bafel's feet as we sprinted through machine gun fire.

I very suddenly started to grow massively fatigued and downright ill; breathing was difficult, and I grew nauseous. My Captain yelled into the radio, and then I heard a Jet tearing through the sky again overhead, approaching rapidly from the south. Just as my Captain told the pilot to go ahead and drop the bombs, and the jet's noise grew to a shivering climax, a large group of Kurds from the Green Prong suddenly materialized from over the ridge from the north; the same ridge that he had just directed the pilot to drop bombs on. They were headed towards the kill zone!

We all winced as the pilot dropped bombs across the face of the ridge at "danger close" range to us; no more than 400 meters away. The Green Prong had made it even further across the target area of the ridge.

Boom, Boom, Boom, Boom!

## One Green Beret

The earth shook like a localized earthquake, I could feel the concussion cut through my bones and every organ in my body, and the ringing in my ears grew even louder due to the thunderous, earth shuddering crack of the explosions. I watched from the corner of the building as the mushroom-like explosions detonated near our Green Prong members; so close that the dust and black smoke from the blasts instantly covered them from view. They were so close I assumed many of them had to have been killed. I looked at my Captain and his face was made of stone. The wind blew the giant plumes of black smoke slowly to my left in front of the snowy peaks.

Suddenly there was an omnipresent sound of massive amounts of mortar rounds or artillery rounds, screaming and falling through the sky from what seemed like every direction. My blood ran cold as I thought either AAI still had copious mortar tubes somewhere, or that perhaps the Iranians decided to take sides against us (we could see one of their border checkpoints from where we were).

One of the Kurds said something that I did not understand. Bafel translated for us and said "Rocks!" The sounds of mortars and artillery that I thought I heard were the sound of *rocks* that had been launched into the sky at high velocity by the explosive power of the four large bombs that were just dropped.

The AAI machine gun fire stopped. My Captain immediately called the Green Prong, and it turned out that miraculously no one was killed that they knew of. It was almost a major friendly fire incident. There were so few of us, and so many Kurds, and they moved so dynamically that it was nearly impossible to account for where they could be at any given time. Trying to keep track of where they all were was an intractable task. The best approach was to try to stay on the front line with them and spread out among them, but that was not easy to accomplish because in reality the "front line" is measured in miles, and it's not straight, and it has Peshmerga in depth. This is one of the challenges in unconventional warfare using surrogate forces: "command and control" turns into an exercise of continuous accountability using unsophisticated communications in an ad hoc fashion among thousands of guerillas.

The Green Prong Kurds swept southeast along the freshly bombed ridge. They avoided the black scorched holes in the earth that the bombs had created. Their small forms moved so quickly across the rough terrain that from my vantage point they seemed like tiny figurines. There was a bit of sporadic firing, but since the bombs had taken care of most of the AAI there; the firing we heard was just the Kurds making sure the AAI bodies they encountered were dead.

I grew more and more ill by the minute; we'd been fighting since dawn. I had developed a splitting headache and incredible lethargy. We packed everything up, and then began to discuss what we should do next. A small group of Kurds came down the hill behind us in a vehicle and told us they had found some large missiles in a position on a hill. Grit and another guy went to investigate with the Kurds, and quickly came back with information that they had found some very large French made missiles. The missiles were still in the cases.

We were almost completely out of .50 cal ammunition, we were all down to only a few magazines, and it was getting dark. The Kurds are not night fighters for the most part, at least not in rural areas, so we all decided to call it a night and head back down to Sargat to find a place to spend the night. The way I felt, I was glad to call it a day after more than 16 hours of fighting.

As we reentered Sargat, I was stunned to see that Kurds had already occupied most of the village. I saw a few women sweeping out houses and getting ready to move their families into them; they waved and smiled to us thankfully. Kids were already playing outside in some areas, ignoring the dead bodies everywhere. I realized we had just liberated a very large area of Kurdistan from these AAI Extremists. The Kurds were making piles of dead AAI bodies in various places, and their estimates were that we killed at least 300 of them. They wouldn't tell us how many Kurds were wounded or killed.

There were massive amounts of captured AAI information and equipment. The Kurds consolidated it all into the back of pickups and dump trucks. We found a house in the center of the village and hunkered down for the night. Everyone chatted a bit about each other's experiences before going to sleep. Grit's small team had been in serious trouble much like mine had. The medic with Grit had tried to patch up a Kurd whose intestines were hanging out, and there were many other details exchanged. I felt so bad I just tried to sleep. In hindsight I think those 106 rounds had given me a serious concussion.

The next morning, still feeling awful, I awoke to find our Battalion and Group commander had arrived at our house in Sargat. Colonel Cleveland and Ltc Tovo had come out to see how we were doing and congratulate us on a job well done. We shook hands and I gave Col Cleveland a man hug. I had known Col Cleveland for quite some time, he was my Battalion commander on my trip to Bihać Bosnia, and I'd always had a good rapport with him. We told them our stories, they patted our backs, and they told us what was going on in the big picture of the war. Soon they left, but their acknowledgment and opinion that we had done a good job made our spirits soar.

After Tovo and Cleveland departed, a Sensitive Site Exploitation (SSE) team arrived to look for evidence of chemical weapons production in the Sargat chemical facility. Some of the members of this SSE team wore those silver, shiny chemical protective suits. As we watched them, we half-jokingly asked ourselves why weren't *we* wearing these shiny space suits the day prior as we walked through and then ate lunch right next to the chemical facility? What kind of intelligence had these guys received that we didn't? Having no alternative, I brushed it off and escorted them to the facility, then poked around for a while with them in the cool early morning air. There were scattered stones, rubble, and equipment everywhere.

A representative from the SSE team said they needed hair samples from the dead AAI fighters, because hair sample analysis would be one of the ways to prove whether AAI had been performing chemical and poison engineering in the facility. This request trickled down to my medic and I, and we were told to go cut hair samples from the dead AAI bodies that were littered throughout the valley. We were told to place the hair samples into zip lock bags, take a picture of each body from which we had cut the hair using a digital camera, then label each bag of hair with the corresponding photo name.

My medic and I looked at each other in disbelief, and we set out on foot with a few Kurds towards the north side of Sargat to get the job done. I immediately arrived at the edge of a seemingly endless expanse of dead and disfigured human bodies.

## One Green Beret

The first dead person I encountered was severely burned. His lips were burnt off one side of the mouth along with most of his face. This created a horrifying snarl expression, because his teeth and burnt gums were exposed only on one side. The combination of the ghastly snarl, the burnt and wrinkled black eyes that seemed to peer through my soul, the smell of his burnt flesh, and the contorted frozen expression on his face seemed almost supernatural to me. I reached out and grabbed his hair, *touched his hair*, and snipped some off. I was so close to him I could see individual gnarled facial hairs protruding from the pores of his lifeless skin. His head wobbled a bit like an unstable inanimate object in a hideous, abnormal way, unresponsive to my touch. I was sickened as I stuffed the hair into a plastic bag; almost forgot to breath as I stood over the corpse, and then I continued through the rolling hills of death before me that were littered with motionless mangled corpses. I think I confirmed the existence of Hell this day.

There was a group of 5 bodies that had been charred and melted together into a heap of gore; almost like a pile of slightly melted and burned human wax figures. The pile was mostly blackened, but also consisted of twisted skin and sizzled human fat, burnt clothing and equipment, and exposed and broken bones and entrails. One man's abdomen was burned through, so his intestines had spilled out and were also charred. The motionlessness of their bodies and eyes was indescribable. Their mouths were agape under empty, burned eye sockets, and they wore perpetual expressions of pain and agony. It was as if a demented artist had erected a monument to horror. The level of anxiety I felt as I approached the pile made my entire body go so numb and tingly that I could barely feel myself.

One of the Kurds said the pile of men had been hit with a 106mm round; I guessed it was an incendiary round because that's the only thing that could have burned them to death so fast that they couldn't separate in time, hence causing the *merging via melting* that I stood there looking at in awe. As I got close enough to cut some hair, the smell of burnt flesh was staggering as I inhaled their fumes. I cut some hair off the ones that actually still had small patches of hair left; crispy flesh fell off in some places because of the movement when I grabbed...touched...felt... the hair in order to cut it. I was careful not to pull too hard on the hair to extend it so I could cut it, because I didn't want to pull the partially encrusted scalp off with it, and if the hair was singed, I didn't want to break it. It was very difficult to force myself to touch them, and at one point I almost passed out from forgetting to breathe again.

Another had blown himself up with a suicide bomb vest. Some of the AAI had strapped themselves with explosives so they could blow us up if we overran them during the battle. This guy was one example and he'd blown himself in half. Entrails, dark red, with small clumps of dirt stuck to them, mangled and slightly burned, were hanging out of his lower torso and broken twisted legs. So much blood had drained from this half of his body that there was a coagulated trail of sticky darkness extending probably 50 feet down the slope we were standing on. It was a seemingly impossible amount of blood; surreal. The body smelled like shit because of the exploded and exposed intestines dangling out of the torso. The whole area smelled like shit because of the scattered pieces of intestines that were spread around the area from the blast.

Some of his upper shoulders and head, attached to broken, shredded, and burned arms with bones extruding in fragments from them, were about 20 feet uphill. One side of his ribcage was ripped open and protruded upward like some kind of monster's claw, draped in shredded meat. The face, mouth gaping and impossibly crooked, with dead eyes facing different directions, was perverted into a bizarre unnatural expression, and the horrifyingly demented position of the head evinced a brutally broken neck. He had those same relentless, motionless eyes. He still had some good hair, so I kneeled down, grabbed some and cut it. It's impossible to convey or describe the emotion elicited by being inches away from, and touching, mutilated dead human bodies like this. Horror is the only word that comes to mind, but that word still fails to deliver the magnitude of the sentiment that overcame me.

Another brutalized corpse was smashed into a small aqueduct that ran laterally across the ridge. His face was completely concave like a bowl; pushed inward all the way back to the *back of the inside* of his skull, similar to how a deflated soccer ball can be pushed into itself. This made his eyes bizarrely face each other, and stare past each other. Brains, grey and chunky, and a large pool of black coagulated blood were splattered underneath the broken and twisted neck, and upper body. I tried to imagine how this could have happened but could not completely figure it out. I bent down, put my left knee on the ground, then swung my right leg over his body onto the other side of the small aqueduct, hence straddling the carcass. I looked deeply into his frozen concave and sparsely bearded face, and into those open but empty eyes. I drew a shuddering breath as I mustered up the courage to reach down closer to cut off some of his hair. It was difficult to cut, because it was like most of the hair was inside of a bowl. I pulled the hair pretty hard to detach the skin from the skull slightly so I could get the scissors inside the bowl enough to cut off a decent amount from the area above his forehead. It made a sickening wet ripping sound as I pulled the skin from the skull. I cut the hair, then I slipped as I was getting up from the straddle position with the hair in one hand and scissors in the other, and I got some blood and brains on my hand as well as my fingerless black leather gloves.

One body was still bleeding somehow, very slowly. A Kurd standing over the corpse explained that this bleeding AAI terrorist had killed his brother during the attack. The Kurd poked the body with his barrel, holding the AK by the pistol grip. The way he poked the body was as if he was simply poking a piece of meat and he did it with no expression on his face or any indication of emotion whatsoever. This is when I fully understood how numb the Peshmerga are to the brutality of war. I cut the hair and kept moving forward, wading through the filth.

We cut hair and took pictures most of the day, switching places at times. The images are all still vivid in my mind. A head that had been savagely ripped off was on the ground with no sign of a body anywhere near it, a seemingly impossible scenario; we cut its hair. A body was blown in half the long way from crotch to neck, peeled apart into a heart shape with the head in the middle; we cut the hair. Legs on the ground. Arms on the ground. Fingers. Feet. Hands. Sections of spinal columns. Meaty ribcages. Skull shards with patches of hair. Fragments of bone and skin and randomly distributed chunks of muscle meat. The smell of burnt hair and flesh and shit and gunpowder permeated the air. Everywhere I looked across the expanse before me, hundreds of yards in any direction, a view of something awful could not be escaped. Death was maddeningly and inescapably everywhere and literally made my head spin.

Finally, we ran out of plastic bags, so we silently walked back through Hell holding dozens of zip lock bags full of hair samples and a digital camera, down to the house we had stayed the night in. We hadn't even put a dent in the number of dead bodies there were in terms of collecting hair samples, but at least it was over.

Imagine looking across 100 football fields and seeing a mangled dead body or cluster of dead bodies lying every five yards across the entire expanse. It was like a scene out of some absurd zombie apocalypse movie. The Kurds were throwing bodies into trucks like cordwood towards the end of the day. I was stunned at how mechanically they did it. They had to get the bodies out of there somehow since Kurdish families were already moving into houses in Sargat, and to do it effectively they just had to stop feeling anything. The Kurds have spent generations in war; they had it down to a science.

We found passports from countries all over the world on the dead bodies and in the buildings in Sargat. They hailed from multiple North African countries, Iran, Syria, Saudi Arabia, Lebanon, Turkey, Afghanistan, and there was even a member of the PLO there from Palestine, and that's just a few.

We had just made more room for the Kurds to live in peace (as much as they ever could I guess), and we got rid of a bunch of psychos in this corner of Iraq. I kept telling myself this over and over to rationalize what I'd just experienced.

We spent another day in the Halabja area, firing rockets and mortars at members of AAI as they escaped into Iran. The sound of the Katooshas and mortars became maddening; every time one fired all the fibers in my body tensed. I watched many dozens of AAI in the distance climbing over the snow packed peaks along the border on foot; black specs moved across the white peaks that pointed high into the huge blue sky over Iran. Periodically, the Iranian border positions also fired at them as they tried to get into Iran. Because of the immense terrain, most of them got away.

As I watched so many AAI fighters escape into the mountains, I felt surprised, when I realized the reality that we hadn't actually killed them all. Did we succeed? Then I thought about where they'd pop up next, and I couldn't help but wonder whether what we had just done had been pointless or not. If there had been approximately one thousand AAI, and we'd killed about 300 of them, then where did the rest of them go and what would they do next? How many had already fled days or weeks before the impending attack, and where did they go? I didn't have time or energy to deeply contemplate these questions. We eventually said goodbye to the PUK in Halabja; they said we fought like tigers. We drove to the Kurdish Headquarters at ASW to receive our next mission.

Operation Viking Hammer exposes a key challenge in counter terrorism; the perception that going after them will actually do any good or not; and opinions vary (rightfully so). Terrorists don't have a nationality, they follow no laws, borders don't exist to them, and they can easily melt safely into the population (because they know we will never target the civilian population). So, direct attacks on them aren't always very effective long term, they just cause dispersion, morphing, reorganization, then reemergence. "Whack a mole" as a military tactic is unsustainable, but often the only option (if one feels compelled to do anything at all). What would have happened if we had never routed AAI? Would they have built something horrible in the Sargat facility? Would they have faded away?

One Green Beret

Would AQI and ISIS have formed if AAI hadn't been dispersed? We'll never know.

    We prepared to head out towards the Green Line to take on the Iraqi Army.

## Chapter 8
### Tuz, Iraq
### The Green Line

After Viking Hammer, we drove to the PUK Peshmerga headquarters near the As Sulaymaniyah airstrip, where we had lived during most of the AFO mission; it had become the Headquarters for my Battalion (3$^{Rd}$ Battalion 10$^{th}$ Special Forces Group), and the war was in full motion. I was impressed by the energy at the headquarters as I watched thousands of Peshmerga and Green Berets rushing around as we drove through the gate. We acquired a fresh supply of ammunition and we received new Land Rovers; the four door Defender model.

We stayed for a few hours, and I quickly ate some baklava and caught up with one of my German speaking Peshmerga friends. My team leadership was given new orders, and soon we departed for our Company Headquarters, which was located on the north side of the village of Cham Chamal.

After a short drive south, we arrived at my Company headquarters to find that it was only slightly more advanced than a shack. It was a dilapidated concrete block building that was nestled into the north side of a steep ridge, very well protected from any potential Iraqi rocket or mortar fire from the Green Line. My company commander, the same very calm and collected intellectual who led our infiltration into Iraq for the AFO mission, met us out front waving and looking positive. We all shook his hand with a smile, and he told us what a great job we'd done against AAI. Then he brought us inside the concrete shack to tell us what we needed to do.

We stood in a semi-circle in a dingy and dimly lit little room facing a map that was clumsily taped to the peeling wall. I could smell our collective body odor since we hadn't taken a shower in about two weeks, and I still didn't feel quite right. My team's mission was to go south into the unknown and somehow locate and link up with an element of about 5000 randomly dispersed Peshmerga, then conduct bombing and harassing missions against the two tank brigades of Iraqi military (after figuring out where they were), and then eventually attack the city of Tuz. He pointed to a massive area east of Kirkuk and north of Tuz on the huge map. He told us that while we operated in the Tuz area, the rest of the company was going to seize Kirkuk with about twenty thousand Peshmerga.

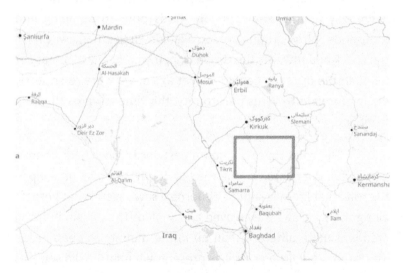

*My ODA's approximate sector (Map source: OpenStreetMap)*

He also told us that some conventional Airborne unit had flown through ultra-secure airspace and parachuted into a massively secure Airstrip up in the Kurdish KDP sector somewhere, and we all wondered why they hadn't just landed on the airstrip – 10th SF Group guys could have organized a picnic or something for them. We assumed they were just trying to get a mustard stain.

My commander reminded us that the whole reason for the Task Force Viking northern front was to harass the Iraqi Army enough so they would not go south to fight against our main attack force that was headed for Baghdad. I wondered why we didn't take all the Kurds into Baghdad to become the main effort *ourselves*, rather than the conventional forces. We made a quick plan, our commander wished us luck, and we headed southeast.

I had no idea where we were going, other than we were going to an area north of Tuz, to drive around with the hope of eventually finding some friendly Kurds prior to bumping into thousands of Iraqi troops. As we rolled down the road away from the shack and towards the Green Line, my company commander faded in the distance behind us. Yet again, we were relentlessly driving forward towards uncertainty, this time towards the Iraqi front line.

The road that shot south-eastward from Cham Chamal was awful. We named it "the road of doom" after we hit a dip in the road that literally sent us airborne. I saw several goat herders along the way, and they waved and smiled. The terrain in this d area was quite different than up in the mountains deep inside Kurdistan. Very little grass was present, what little I did see was brown. There were wadis with flat stones and light brown sandy dirt, and it looked like what I expected to see on the outskirts of a desert. We drove very nervously for several hours, we didn't know if we could trust anyone, so we were careful not to rush up on strangers who were also driving on the roads. It was entirely possible that around every corner we might run right into an entire thousands-strong Iraqi Army unit, because I really didn't know where anything was. Finally, after a few very tenuous hours, I saw a line of vehicles up ahead that looked like Peshmerga, but I wasn't sure.

We drove past the line of vehicles, I was ready for a gunfight at any moment, until finally we arrived at a small cluster of reddish clay buildings. When we pulled up, about fifty Peshmerga came out of the huts and met us with smiles; I immediately felt more secure (not all Kurds could automatically be considered friendly, there were many factions of Kurds). My team sergeant and Captain got out with our interpreter and talked to them for a bit. Everyone seemed positive, and apparently, they told my leadership where we needed to go to centralize ourselves in respect to how the Peshmerga were generally distributed across our enormous area of responsibility. We took off again and followed a few random Peshmerga vehicles.

Finally, after driving though windy roads past hundreds of abandoned Iraqi bunkers and positions, over militarized hilltops covered in razor wire and interlocking trenches and straddling some tank mines that were dug into the road, we reached an area where there was a small rectangular one-story building on the left side. It had a flat roof, and in the area behind the building there were large amounts of pipes and pumps that covered about a 200-meter square area, which made a crude foreground to an endless expanse of desolate, flat, dry terrain under a massive blue sky. There was also another building in the same area, about one hundred meters to our left. The immediate surroundings were largely rock, sand, and randomly dispersed tufts of brownish grass. I kept thinking that every building we saw might have been some kind of chemical weapons depot for

WMD. Part of me hoped we'd be the ones who found the smoking gun. This building would be our new home for a while, so we set up our satellite radio communications and established a security plan. Within minutes, we discovered Peshmerga had occupied the other building, and they came over with tea.

The Peshmerga explained the situation to a few of us, and what they'd been doing. They had spread out into dozens, possibly hundreds, of tiny teams, and they were conducting harassing attacks against the Iraqi Army on the outskirts of both Tuz and Kirkuk (and ultimately across the entire Green Line, which had been pushed south). They were using the wadis and the terrain to get close to the Iraqi front line. They were excited to see us start calling in air strikes on the highly vulnerable Iraqi units they had observed. The Peshmerga told us the Iraqi military had occupied a large ridge just northeast of Tuz, and they were dug in all along the road that led northwest from Tuz to Kirkuk. It was our responsibility to kill them.

After a sleepless night, the next day we began operations. We had a very simple job: go find the Iraqi Military, bring some Kurds for security, and call in air strikes. We slept only a short distance from the front line of tens of thousands of Iraqi troops, and it only took a half hour or less, moving over rough terrain, to get close enough to see hundreds of them with the naked eye. I developed a permanent eerie feeling when I looked at the map and realized that tens of thousands of enemy troops were right up the road, and we didn't have dedicated air support and only a handful of anti-tank weapons. They could have dropped artillery on us or overran us easily if they'd known where we were, so we were prepared for that to happen at any moment.

On my first patrol out to the Green Line, to attack the Iraqi units, we drove with the Kurds in one of their pickup trucks. I jumped up and smiled to them all as I crammed myself into the back of a pickup between a few smelly Peshmerga who had dirty faces, dark suntans, and they were constantly grinning at me from under their black and white headwraps. One of them pointed up in the air and kept smiling and saying "siarra, siarra." He then reached out and grabbed the antenna that stuck out of my radio pouch and pointed at the sky again, and made some bomb dropping and explosion sounds. Siarra meant "aircraft," and they were very excited to see what American aircraft could do. They would not be disappointed.

I thought to myself, "here I go again," as I bounced down a dusty dirt road, moving towards the unknown in the back of a primitive truck full of smiling Kurds, headed towards the enemy. The trucks slowed down after quite a few dusty and bumpy minutes, and the Kurds chattered quietly and restlessly. I dismounted with a clatter, and I continued on foot in a southerly direction surrounded by the small team of Peshmerga, towards the Iraqi front line, concealed within the low, sandy, and dry wadi floor. We rounded many corners and traversed a few small knolls. I was getting very close to the ridgeline that was just to the north of Tuz, where hundreds, maybe thousands of enemy Iraqi soldiers were.

The Kurds chattered to each other and pointed upwards, then started climbing up a small hill to my left front. As they got to the top, they began crawling so they wouldn't silhouette themselves. I took out my spotting scope from my small pack and followed them up. I was also with one other Green Beret from my team as well and our Air Force Special Tactics (STS) guy. I stayed low and crawled into place next to the Peshmerga. I laid in the prone position and looked south towards the massive tan and blue expanse of the Green Line. The view was alarming.

Without even using the high-powered spotting scope, I observed Iraqi Army positions for as far left and right as my eyes were capable of perceiving. The enemy was sprawled in front of us for literally as far as I could see; as if they constituted the actual horizon. There were trucks, antennae, buildings, cars, hundreds of soldiers walking around, bunkers, uniformed Iraqi soldiers standing in formation, and far to my right-front there was a road with some military vehicles driving up and down it. I was about 1000 meters away, which was very close in this open terrain. From the distance, the scene looked like a military version of a giant ant farm under an endless desert sky; I felt tiny in contrast. I started looking at specifics through the spotting scope.

I focused the scope on an individual soldier who was half exposed, standing in what appeared to be a foxhole, quite a distance away from the rest of his unit – closer to us. His movements indicated a bit of boredom and misery to me. I could almost see his facial expressions through the spotting scope, and he was easily visible with the naked eye. When I was an infantryman, I had been in similar situations to his (before I joined the Green Berets), except in my experience it was just training. I remembered how oppressive it was to stand in a foxhole for days or weeks on end, and I was quite sure that it's a completely different, and a much worse experience, when you are waiting for the United States Air Force to drop bombs on you. His green helmet casted a shadow over half of his young, tan face, and I think he was talking to himself. I used to talk to myself when I was in a foxhole too.

Our STS guy called for AWACS on the radio, and within the hour a jet was "inbound" for our usage. As the aircraft approached, the Kurds started to get very excited, and the Iraqis started to scurry before me as the seemingly omnipresent crackling noise in the sky increased. It looked like someone had tapped on the ant farm's glass, or shaken it. That lone soldier ducked down into his foxhole and disappeared below the surface, all that was left was a tiny dark hole in the brown earth. I took note that there were still dozens of soldiers on the road in front of a cliff along the ridge in front of Tuz when the bombs hit.

The concussions from the bombs were unimaginably vicious; the bombs must have been bigger than the ones they dropped during Viking Hammer. They produced god-like cracks of thunder that shook the earth; shock waves permeated my intestines and skull even though we were 1000 meters away. Massive amounts of dust, flame, and black smoke curled hundreds of feet into the big sky like nebulous skyscrapers. I thought deeply for a second about what it must be like to be one of those tiny Iraqis down there; the horror. The noise from the blasts dissipated into the distance while I watched a brutal scene unfold through a gap in the dust and smoke.

A large chunk of the north side of the cliff above where the Iraqis were standing on the road collapsed from the blast. Through my spotting scope I watched clearly as a huge avalanche of rock and sand buried at least a dozen of the soldiers alive; they made futile attempts to escape their fate, but they were overcome in an instant. I forgot to breathe for so long that blackness swept into my vision as my oxygen depleted, and I almost passed out. I actually forgot to breathe. Every muscle in my body became so tense that my jaw cramped, and muscle spasms rippled through my thighs and trapezoids. As the wind blew the black clouds that still hung over the Iraqis to my left and dissipated, my tunnel vision faded as I regained my breath. I then noticed there were dozens of dark human forms laying on the ground around where each of the bombs had hit; motionless, dead.

Through the spotting scope I could almost see the burnt faces of the dead, and of course after the haircutting in Sargat I had plenty of material for my imagination to generate a clear picture of what those dead and mutilated Iraqi soldiers looked like down there.

While we waited for more aircraft for another several hours, the Iraqis meandered around, and I assumed they were trying to figure out what to do with all the dead people. They started consolidating the dead as we decided to return to our compound. Just before I crawled backwards off the hill, I focused my scope on that one lone Iraqi's foxhole. He stood back up and adjusted his green helmet, then continued to talk to himself.

We continued to operate like this for several weeks, which seemed like an eternity. We basically ran shifts, and continuously bombed the Iraqis with immeasurable brutality. The Iraqi soldiers were not attacking us and didn't really seem to pose much of a threat, yet we were still doing our job and killing them. On one occasion they fired some artillery at us, but usually they were just sitting there out in the open, powerless against our aircraft and guided munitions, facing imminent death. I felt like a kid standing in front of an ant farm with a giant magnifying glass.

## One Green Beret

One night, over tea, as we talked about the day's events with the Kurds, they told us that the Iraqi military officer leadership was actually killing their own soldiers because some of the soldiers were trying to run away to escape inevitable death. If this information was true, we were bombing Iraqi soldiers who were being forced by their officer leadership to sit there and die. Moreover, by proxy, the officers were forcing themselves to die as well.

One time while I was out on an observation post (OP), I heard small arms fire from where the Iraqis were, and I imagined that the shots fired were from Iraqi officers killing their men for trying to leave. From that point on, when I was on an OP, I stopped watching the bombs drop. I looked away or put my head down after we told the pilots "you're cleared hot."

My Captain and I had a conversation late one night. He introduced me to the notion that it would have been strategically better if we dropped leaflets to encourage the Iraqi soldiers to surrender, rather than dropping bombs on them. I was glad I wasn't the only one feeling like what we were doing was not optimal. If we kept killing all the soldiers, then who would become the new Iraqi security forces when the war was over? If we bombed them like this for much longer, would we drive them into the arms of the local terrorist groups? Would they join a dispersed and reconstituted Ansar Al Islam? Why were we doing what we were doing and what was the strategy behind it? We talked about it for a long time that night, and several times after; we cared enough about this idea to propose it to our headquarters.

I threw stones when I was back on radio duty, which made me think of the time I pitched a no-hitter in the Connecticut shoreline baseball championships when I was a kid, and I thought about my family a lot. I read the intelligence summaries (INTSUMs) and situation reports (SITREPs) every day. The SITREP was useful because it told us what everyone else was doing in the war, but the INTSUMs were high level and mostly useless to our operations; our Peshmerga comrades provided much more specific and useful information. We had tea with the Kurds and let them shoot our weapons for fun. We traded stories about the different ways we'd seen Iraqis die along the Green Line. One day our old CIA team buddies showed up and we swapped a few war stories with them.

We dug a slit trench in the side yard, and the smell from it somehow attracted a pack of dogs. The dogs frequently ate our shit. One of the guys on my team named each dog, and we assigned the dogs the collective title of "The Turd Burglars." Some of the dogs were vicious, and they often barked all night. Grit, who had no patience for such things, shot and killed a few of the dogs for barking too much.

During one random conversation, one of the guys on my team suggested that maybe we could just drive right into the Iraqi units' area and try to get them to surrender. He was joking, but after my experiences in Bosnia and Kosovo, I actually think that his idea was not far from an invalid thought. I started to understand what my father meant when he said he always wanted to just go shake the Vietcong's hands because he was sure they could have all just gotten along ok.

One day I called home on a satellite phone. I talked to my father in Connecticut from out in front of our building in Iraq. I told him that everything was ok. He told me to *never think anything is ok during a war* and to not get complacent. It was damn good advice from a Silver Star recipient with three purple hearts (Vietnam). He also told me my wife and daughter were doing ok living with them, but my mom's hair was falling out and my wife had lost almost 20 pounds from the stress of wondering where I was within the craziness they were watching on the news. The news had reported a friendly fire incident involving the Kurds and Special Forces, and they thought it could have been me, and had no easy way to confirm or deny. I hated the stress I was putting them through, and I hoped that I would survive to see them all again.

On one particular rotation out to an OP, I encountered two truckloads of Kurds waiting on the side of the road. I was always very jovial and super friendly to the Kurds, because I genuinely liked and trusted them and I wanted to always keep a good rapport because we needed them, so I asked them if they wanted to come with us. They were all smiles, and with a rattle of weapons and equipment, they loaded up and followed us down the wadis.

We navigated in vehicles for a while, then on foot through the wadis until we were very close to the Iraqis and arrived at a place near the road that led from Tuz to Kirkuk. We got in position and started spotting for targets.

The Air Force STS guy got AWACS on the radio, and we waited. The Kurds made tea behind some cover, and when they were done, they asked us when the aircraft would arrive. They were surprised when I told them that we don't have aircraft dedicated to us, we only got leftovers. I laughed when they told us that they thought every single one of us had our own personal siarra. Then something new happened.

I saw several Iraqi tanks maneuvering, and it looked like they were headed our way.

You have not felt fear until you've seen a military *tank*, an *enemy* tank, moving towards you. A tank is a giant machine that is completely engineered for the sole purpose of war and ultimately the administration of human death. When I saw the tanks, it was equivalent to seeing the grim reaper, and the presence of such evil evoked a familiar, but still immeasurable feeling of doom. My blood ran cold and my nerves almost burst with tingling electricity when I also noticed dozens of large Iraqi 2.5-ton personnel trucks, more tanks, and hundreds of bustling Iraqi soldiers. The Kurds started chattering nervously. When the Kurds got nervous, I got *really* nervous. The STS guy miraculously got an aircraft on call, which was as refreshing to know as it was to finally see the Iraqis become an actual threat.

I overheard the radio as I laid next to the STS guy, and I could hear the pilot talking. Not only were there a few Iraqi tanks driving around in front of us, there were also many tanks dug into the ground. The jet pilot told us he was going to use a technique called "high angle strafe." "High angle strafe" is when the pilot soars straight up in the air over the target, then drops straight down nose first and fires the chain guns onto the top of their prey. Buried tanks, also called "revetted," are not vulnerable to indirect surface blasts, but their tops are completely exposed to high angle strafe.

The pilot flew with an almost sinister form of elegance, far up into the massive sky until the aircraft became a silver spec on what looked like the edge of the atmosphere. The aircraft seemingly hovered for an instant, and then slowly and gracefully fell into a nose-dive. Violent bursts from the main gun completely pummeled the revetted tanks and the ground around them. Each round produced three sounds in rapid succession; the bark of the shot, the streaming of the round towards the ground, then the thud of when the round hit the target. These three sounds happened at the rate of thousands of rounds per minute, which produced violence at imperceptible scale. The roar of the main gun provided foreground for the immense sound of the jet ripping through the giant Iraqi sky. The plane's methodical up and down movements reminded me of a music conductor's hand, but instead of music there was the sound of jet engines mixed with the burp of the machine gun, and the result was death rather than a melody.

After the aircraft had finished its relentless strafing runs and ran out of ammunition, dozens of tendrils of black smoke rose from the scorched kill zone. The wind moved the slender swaying tendrils of smoke to my left in unison, and they looked like hundreds of giant morphing apparitions as the wind changed their shapes, until they finally dissipated at random across the massive landscape. There were still thousands of Iraqi soldiers out there in front of me as we packed up and walked away.

When I got back to the refinery, I immediately discovered that the Iraqis had not been maneuvering on us. They were preparing to move south out of the area. I was disappointed but didn't have time to contemplate. My Captain said we were going to attack and occupy Tuz immediately, *that very minute*, with about three to five thousand Peshmerga. The rest of my company was already on the move to seize Kirkuk with another massive Peshmerga horde.

In less than ten minutes we were packed and ready to go. I was one of the drivers that night. I did not look forward to driving, especially since it was growing dark, and my eyes caused me even more trouble at night than they did normally. I took a deep breath, grasped the steering wheel tightly, depressed the accelerator, and my vehicle lurched forward towards Tuz and yet another unknown set of dangerous circumstances. Within a few minutes it became pitch dark, and we encountered a large convoy of random vehicles full of Peshmerga spread out for about a mile along the road.

They had 2.5-ton green trucks, jeeps, land rovers, motorcycles, and some had cars or taxi cabs; the scene was quite similar to the assembly of Peshmerga for Operation Viking Hammer: total chaos. I drove behind my Captain's Land Rover, past dozens of vehicles and cheering Kurds, and he was behind a Kurdish 2.5-ton truck. Some Kurdish trucks joined our convoy, and I drove with them for about a half an hour in the same general direction as usual.

For several hours, I followed blurry rear headlights in the blackness and watched the ambient light barely penetrate the darkness and bounce off fractals of stone and sand in my peripheral vision. I felt like I was on an expedition through the dark side of the moon. We moved along rocky wadis and then through extremely rough terrain that I hadn't been through before. I had no idea where we were, and soon I heard weapons fire popping in the distance. The weapons fire quickly grew from sporadic to continuous as we grew closer to the outskirts of Tuz. We reached the top of a rise that provided a vantage point over the road that led from Kirkuk into Tuz.

On the road below me about a kilometer to my right, I saw hundreds of Iraqi military vehicles on the dark road with their headlights on for as far as I could see. The lights were backdropped by complete darkness, so the meandering line of lights looked like a giant miles-long snake floating in deep space. The road looked like it was completely packed all the way from Tuz to Kirkuk. The Iraqis were indeed leaving Kirkuk and Tuz, and it looked like *all of them*. We pressed forward, and I thought we'd be in a serious battle with the Iraqis in a few minutes. However, just as I left that vantage point, something unforgettable happened.

The Kurdish truck in front of us was suddenly hit by an explosion.

We were in a minefield.

Everyone stopped. The truck in front of us was smoking, and the front of it was mangled. The Peshmerga were yelling frantically. My mind went wild with fear, and my heart pounded as my body became overrun with tension and anxiety like I'd been hit with a stun gun. The Kurds walked around with flashlights, jabbering incessantly in urgent pitched voices. White light from Kurds with flashlights danced across the rocky and sandy terrain and their voices grew more and more intense. They found mines everywhere. They even found many mines *behind us*, which meant we'd been lucky we made it as far as we had. This also meant there was no turning back; it was just as dangerous to go back as it was to go forward, and because of the terrain, and the darkness of the night, it would have been impossible to perfectly retrace our steps.

The Kurds asked us if we had anything that they could use to mark the mines. Luckily, we had several boxes of mini chemlights, so we passed them out. The Kurds, and some of my teammates, got out of the land rovers, very carefully, and started marking the mines (that they could find) using flashlights to carefully place chemlights next to each mine. The plan was to drive forward and straddle the chemlights and everyone would stay in line. There was nothing else we could do.

It was pitch black. My eyes contorted the glow of the chemlights terribly. The feeling of doom I previously felt from tanks and from being pinned down by machine gun fire was nothing compared to the spirit-crushing feeling that hit me as I released the clutch, depressed the gas, and continued onward through the minefield. Thinking became pointless after a few minutes, and I expected to be ripped to shreds at every moment as I straddled the blurry chemlights. I continuously squinted my eyes in a futile attempt to make the chemlights clearer and hoped like hell that if I did run over a mine that it would at least kill me instantly and not leave me mangled. I had no idea how far we had to go to reach the end of this minefield, and there was no guarantee that we had marked all the mines; I expected to become red mist at every nanosecond, and the feeling of stress was unimaginable. I could not imagine anything less glorious than being killed by a landmine.

I drove like this *all night*. My jaw began to ache, and I realized it was because I had been clenching my teeth in anticipation of being blown up for so many hours. When we ran out of chem lights, the Kurds started reusing the ones from behind us. Eventually, hours later we made it out of the minefield and into the outskirts of Tuz. I was glad when we reached pavement. We moved through an area where we were surrounded by a large volume of weapons fire. The Kurds said that the fighting was *not Kurds against the Iraqis*. I didn't understand. If it wasn't the Kurds fighting the Iraqis, then who was fighting who?

We eventually made it to an actual road. I was too tired and emotionally bludgeoned to feel relieved that we were out of the minefield. It was still dark, and we pulled into someone's house in Tuz. A very friendly Kurd invited us into his house, led us into a musty and dark room with low ceilings and concrete walls, and then gave us tea and bread. We were told we would hide there until the battles were over.

Early in the morning, way before daylight broke, when I was the only one awake, still painfully tense, a little Kurdish girl, probably 4 or 5 years old, came to the doorway of her living room in a simple tan sleeping dress, where my team was sleeping amongst our piles of kit. When I turned my weary head to look at her tiny form standing in the doorway, she just stood there in the dim light and stared at me with big and curious dark eyes. Her face wore a surprisingly intense expression that I oddly perceived as what appeared to be *hope*. I smiled big and gently waved my fingerless black gloved hand, trying to be as small and friendly looking as a dirty and unshaven, six foot three, 225 pound, traumatized, American Green Beret possibly could. She smiled back, gripped her dress anxiously, and her big dark eyes lit up with pure joy; simply because I turned out to be nice. She gave me a very shy and microscopic wave, and then she turned and dashed away down the hall and out of sight; seemingly delighted. I thought of my baby daughter, and I imagined she would have been just as curious and hopeful for niceness if there were suddenly a bunch of Peshmerga laying in *her* living room one night. That little girl gave me a burst of motivation, and I swore to myself again that I would make it out of Iraq alive to see my family.

I slept for an hour at most, and at sunset my Captain and Grit went outside to figure out what to do next. They came back in with news that we were going to stay with a Peshmerga unit near the center of Tuz. We said goodbye to the owner of the house, I looked for the little girl to say goodbye, but I couldn't find her.

We left and drove down a paved road towards the center of Tuz. We passed blown up tanks and cars, and I watched Kurds scavenging material from everywhere and everything. Some people towed Anti-Aircraft guns with Taxi cabs, and others drove tanks. I kept staring numbly at the dead human beings laying in contorted positions, strewn about the sides of the road like trash. One body had been completely flattened like a bug, complete with guts squirting out, by a tank. As we drove towards the center of Tuz, I noticed that various groups of people had raised flags of all different types randomly throughout the city, and there were men with guns, *armed militants*, generally assembled around where each of the flags were. I was surprised to see so many different opposing groups.

I was tired as hell when we arrived at our new home, which was a compound of deteriorating buildings surrounded by a crude block wall about 5 feet high. When I looked around as one naturally does, I guessed the compound had been a school or a small Iraqi Army barracks. I unloaded my gear and established myself in a narrow one-story rectangular building with many empty window openings. The Kurdish leadership for the area came to our building and gave us an update on the situation.

One Green Beret

They informed us that the siege of Kirkuk and Tuz were over. However, I was surprised when they told us that over 16 different militant, political, ethnic, and tribal groups had occupied Tuz, and they were all fighting for territory. This information explained all the different flags I'd seen flying as we drove in, as well as the fighting I had heard while driving through the minefield. Even the Islamic Group of Kurdistan (IGK) had secured a spot.

The next day we decided to explore the ridge that we had repetitively bombed in the weeks prior to invading Tuz. We drove up to the top of the ridgeline, near where all those Iraqis had been buried in the avalanche. The terrain was like a rocky desert, like a wasteland, and there were Iraqi military uniforms and equipment strewn across the brown and reddish landscape for as far as I could see. I could see for miles to the north and northeast once we reached the top of the ridge. The terrain looked like a sea of sand and rock, and veins of wadis extended out to the horizon line. I peered northeastward, towards where we used to sit in the OPs to call air strikes. I realized as I perceived the enormous expanse below me, that it was no wonder the Iraqis could never see us; we would have been mere specks on this moonlike landscape. The most memorable aspect of exploring this thoroughly bombed ridge was when we approached what looked like a horse, or a donkey, I couldn't tell anymore.

The once-beautiful animal, a female, was laying on its side, barely alive. She had almost no skin left on the side of her body that was facing up, and the skin that was left was burned severely. Her eyes were burned almost completely out, and her ears were burnt off. What was left of her eyes was blackened and twisted, or had a hideous veil of what appeared to be burnt cornea. Her teeth were exposed as a snarl due to most of her lips having been burnt off in a similar way as the dead AAI fighter I had cut hair from a month prior. Although those things were horrific, the part that shocked and bothered me the most was the state of the poor animal's legs, which were hopelessly shredded. Each leg looked as if it had been flayed and the bone had been removed, and then the sheath of skin and muscle that should have surrounded the bone had been cut crudely the long way into ribbons, except these ribbons consisted of charred reddish meat, which gave the animal the appearance of some kind of demented monster. The poor thing kept trying to stand because our movement had scared her, she could probably smell and hear us but not see us. She kept flapping her brutalized legs, the shards slapped against the ground in a terrible way and made a sort of splat sound, and she was producing a dreadful version of a neigh due to her damaged face. Since I am basically an animal loving country boy at heart who grew up around eastern Connecticut farms, this visualization was vile and heartbreaking. The degree of sadness I felt for that completely innocent animal surprised me, a victim of war and perhaps one of our airstrikes. One of the guys on my team shot her in the head with his pistol to put her out of her misery.

Shortly after our arrival in Tuz, the US declared that hostilities were over. The war was over. In the Kurdish areas there was infinite rejoicing. When we went across the street to buy food, we encountered a barrage of statements from people like "We love George Bush!" and "Bush Good!" To the Kurds we were heroes. However, the Kurds also thought the idea that the war was suddenly "over" was downright silly.

Our command told us that since the war was now over, we had a new mission. Our new mission was to link up with the different factions within the vicinity of Tuz, and report what was going on in order to provide situational awareness. We switched from all-out war to a peacekeeping mission in one instant. The drastic and abrupt change in mission was actually quite logical, what else could we have done at this point?

The next day my Warrant Officer and I drove around the city of Tuz to perform our new mission, just the two of us along with an interpreter. I was reminded of my time as a JCO in post-war Bosnia, driving around freely, and observing how the normal people, the innocent bystanders of war, went about their business trying to deal with the aftermath of the hell they had just experienced. Frustrated women swept out houses while kids played outside, and men spoke to each other emotionally in the streets. I imagined what it would be like to be in their shoes, to have your entire world turned upside down. Some people waved to us, some just watched us go by.

As we randomly patrolled the streets just to see the state of Tuz and to get a feel for what had materialized, I saw the flag of IGK along the dirty grey road in the distance up ahead. The flag was inside of a small fenced compound with armed and bearded fighters guarding it. Recall that IGK was a group that let us target Ansar Al Islam during our AFO mission, but we had also targeted *them*. We had killed over one hundred of them in their headquarters in Khurmal. Since the war was over, my Warrant Officer insisted we try to meet with them to see what they were up to. It was as if one moment it was our job to kill them, and the next it was our job to chat over tea.

We stopped in front of the IGK compound, parked, and since they didn't shoot at us immediately, we got out of our SUV and approached their compound. When we stepped out of the land rover, wearing US Army uniforms, the facial expressions on the IGK guards became tense and confused. As we approached, I tried my best not to look confrontational, and the two bearded IGK men chatted nervously with each other, but never took their dark eyes off us. I knew they were trying to decide whether they were supposed to kill us or not, so my body tensed in preparation for a gunfight, and I gripped Old Sarge in anticipation. We made it up to where the men stood without them shooting at us, then we asked them if we could speak to their leader. They looked at each other with confusion in their eyes, murmured to each other and shrugged, and one of them turned and walked inside.

Within a few seconds, a thin man with a very robust, dense, shiny, and exceptionally well-maintained black beard walked across the light colored and sun smattered dirt in front of the crude whitewash building to greet us. His AK was slung over his tan equipment, and he had very intense dark eyes that were so deep black they contrasted interestingly with the hue of his light skin. He reminded me, in his face, his clothing, and equipment, like most of the dead AAI fighters I had cut hair from.

Although I was thoroughly ready to kill him, I instinctually extended my hand to him and smiled, and he returned a calm smile back and shook my hand robustly. He invited us to sit down on a small bench in the front of the building. He told someone behind him to bring us all some tea, and we began to talk. I really wasn't surprised that he acted friendly. His first question was exactly what I expected.

"Why did the US bomb IGK in Khurmal?"

I told him the truth; the US bombed IGK because IGK had supported AAI. While the interpreter translated it to the IGK leader I mentally prepared myself for a major gunfight. However, the IGK leader's expression became one of curiosity, and he seemed to think that what I said was a valid explanation. He proceeded to explain that his group was not like AAI, and they had not supported them. Essentially, after a few minutes of him trying to convince us that they were not evil and had not supported AAI, I realized he was just trying to convince us to leave his group alone. Basically, he was passively promising me that they were not a threat, and never would be, probably so we'd think there was no more reason to kill a bunch of them again. Regardless, IGK made some good tea, it tasted a little different than the Kurdish style I was used to. In the back of my mind I kept hoping that the tea was not poisoned as I sipped it. We left on a good note; we didn't think they'd attack us in the near future.

Over the next few weeks, we visited four different Turkmen groups, communist Kurd groups that were not PUK (such as the PKK), and several Arab tribal groups to the west of Tuz. The Arab tribes were interesting to meet. One day I visited a particular tribe that lived in an area that was west of the Tuz airstrip.

We drove west for a couple hours before I pulled up the main road of a desert village that was lined with primitive block and clay dwellings; all very bright with surface reflectance from the harsh sun. The road was bumpy, sandy white, and dusty. We stopped on the right side and got out of the SUV. We met some of the tribal leader's sons in the road. They were cordial and brought us up some stairs on the side of a whitewash house, into a large room, and we all sat cross legged on a carpet on the concrete floor. The room was dimly lit and smelled of tea. A very old man with a white beard, who was more wrinkled than any person I had ever witnessed in my life, constantly did laps around the room in a squatted position, wearing nothing but what amounted to a white loin cloth to cover his frail frame. He had a tea pot in his hand, and he constantly filled tea for everyone. I noticed he had really intense eyes and really gnarly toes when I thanked him for pouring my tea.

I surveyed the half dozen armed men who sat around the edge of the room, facing inwards, legs crossed, with their weapons on the floor beside them. Some of these young men looked deeply into my eyes with earnest, some looked me up and down with curiosity, and some were smiling and nodding their heads as if they wanted to say something but knew I wouldn't have understood their language. I felt an aura of antiquity and wisdom when the leader entered the room and the other men sat up straighter in response, which prompted me to take this situation very seriously. The leader of this group was very old and wrinkled, he sat sternly at the head of the rectangular room, and within a few minutes of casual conversation, he began to ask us about democracy. Our interpreter was terrified.

He asked how democracy worked. I explained the whole concept of voting, and the states, and everything as best I could, the way it is done in America. He had a hard time understanding, and did not like, the logic of "the majority rules." It didn't make sense to him because if his tribe was simply smaller in numbers than any other tribe, then his tribe would inevitably lose in any election, and their interests would not be represented. We talked about it for a while and concluded that he had raised a great point from their perspective. I wasn't in a position where it made sense to try and be overly persuasive. In tribal society, it's very difficult to drop democracy into the mix. He explained that the nature of tribes is high independence, homogeneity, and autonomy, and democracy *across* tribes poses a serious challenge, especially when religious and ethnic dynamics are also in play. I didn't tell him about the electoral college, and I wonder today if that concept would have resonated. He was concerned that without Sadaam keeping the tribes from fighting by ruling with an iron fist, the tribes would digress into complete chaos and warfare over territory and resources, as well as incubate terrorist groups (what we were seeing in Tuz). We eventually left on a friendly note after shaking everyone's hands and thanking them all for the hospitality.

During our stay in Tuz, we had a bit more time on our hands than we had the weeks prior. The Kurds installed an interesting gravity fed outdoor shower for us, and we taught them how to play baseball in the open dirt area inside our small compound. We made massive trash bonfires in the center of the parking area in front of our building. I wrote poems and random stories on whatever paper I could find, and I asked the Kurds if they could find me a guitar anywhere, but they couldn't.

After about two weeks, I became sick with a brutal stomach infection. It was so bad my team medic was on the verge of calling a medevac for me. I was completely incapacitated for about four days. The only thing I was capable of doing was laying in the fetal position next to the filthy hole in the floor bathroom stall as large foreign insects crawled on me, repetitively vomiting and enduring incredible surges in pain from what my medic called "massive fluid shifts" in my intestines. I faded in and out of sleep, while I had nightmares and super intense dreams about the months and weeks prior. If we had been attacked, I don't think I would have been able to fight, that's how sick I was. He gave me two Z-Packs, and I eventually recovered. We also did something kind of strange.

Back in Colorado Springs, there was a great little restaurant called "The Western Omelet" that served the hottest and best tasting green chili in the world. We used to order omelets smothered in this green splendor after our grueling morning exercises. We all missed this place very badly and grew quite wistful about it. In fact, talking about it became sort of a hobby for us once we had all returned back to our house from our daily patrols. One of the guys on my team, who had been a philosophy major in college, decided we should send the restaurant a picture of our team, accompanied by a very nostalgic and elaborately written note. So, we drove out and found a destroyed Iraqi tank along the road to Kirkuk somewhere and we posed for a picture. We stenciled a chili pepper onto the tank first using spray paint and a stencil made from a piece of cardboard, and we also spray-painted "Western Omelet or Bust!" on the tank. We then wrote the letter and printed it along with the picture using our tiny printer we'd been carrying all the while. We asked one of our B-Team guys to figure out the address for us.

The Kurds started to get randomly attacked by various militant groups. The attacks were from mostly Arab groups of different kinds, but some instances of chaos supposedly came from Turkmen groups. We thought this Turkmen problem was interesting, so my Warrant Officer and I again decided to see what some of these Turkmen groups were up to.

There were at least four different splinter groups of Turkmen in town, each had their own compound full of armed fighters. We drove up to the front of one of them at random, parked, and walked right up to the front gate. We smiled and shook hands with the several armed men who were guarding the place, and I asked if we could talk to whoever was in charge. They looked at each other, obviously confused a bit by our level of comfort, shrugged and said OK. They led us through a crowd of dozens of chattering armed men who wore different styles of headgear and clothing, all of which were staring at me inquisitively; I was nervous, but it didn't look like anyone was going to pull a trigger. We continued through a small gate, down a sidewalk, and into a typical concrete building. Inside the building It was quite dark, until we rounded a corner into an area that was better lit, and that's when I saw something interesting.

At first, I thought someone from my own Green Beret unit was standing there in front of us. This guy was in obviously good shape and had what looked like an M4 carbine rifle (the same we used), with a large and interesting scope on it, along with an infrared aiming device of some kind, and a pistol grip under the front handguard. He also had a very fancy and expensive looking black combat vest that was exceptionally well organized and replete with items similar to what we carried. His expensive sunglasses were propped up on the top of his head, over his shiny black, gelled back hair. I realized in a few seconds, that this guy must have been a Turkish Special Forces soldier, and I assumed he might have something to do with the contention between the Kurds and the Turkmen.

Neither one of us knew how to react. I thought to myself: is he the enemy? Will he try to kill me? Should I kill him first? How loyal are these Turkmen to this guy? I was sure by the look on the guy's face that he was asking himself a similar set of questions. No one had provided any guidance on what to do if we encountered Turkish Special Forces, or if they did, I hadn't listened. I didn't know what to do, so I smiled broadly and extended my hand to greet him; I had no desire to invoke a firefight with a few hundred armed Turkmen fighters and a team of Turkish Special Forces. He shook my hand and we both realized we were not a threat to each other. The guy spoke English, and we talked about what a mess Iraq was because of all these factions fighting over the scraps of a now broken country. He explained, in general terms, his mission to make sure the deal that the US made with Turkey that promised the Kurds would leave Kirkuk at some point actually happened. I explained our role as well, and that we were waiting to be replaced by US conventional forces.

He was disappointed that his team wasn't in Kirkuk, because Tuz was a side show for them. I deduced that this guy was like most SOF guys from any country, and he wanted to play in the biggest game he could, which was not Tuz. We chatted for a while about each other's weaponry and equipment. I told him about the night we drove into Tuz through a minefield, and he said his experience getting into Tuz was less exciting. We compared rifles and scopes and I asked him how one goes about becoming a Turkish SF soldier, and we compared that to Green Beret training. He seemed like a good guy who was just there to fulfil an expectation and do his job, like I was. He offered to buy me a drink next time I was in Istanbul. We shook hands and jokingly promised not to kill each other once I left, or at least not unless we had to.

Finally, the conventional forces arrived in Armored vehicles. They bumbled through Tuz, and instantly elicited a feeling of unrest from the people there. My Captain handled all the coordination with them. There were also some Marines nearby, but I think they were near Tikrit. The relationship between us and the conventional forces was awkward, and I wasn't very involved in the collaboration personally.

The Kurds provided us with so much timely information and intelligence, so constantly, that reporting it all, and judging the veracity of it all, became an intractable problem. We attempted to feed the information straight to the conventional troops, but it seemed like they couldn't use intelligence that did not come from their "higher." This meant that they had to wait for our reporting to go up through the echelons and back down for them to actually use it, even though they were *right there with us to begin with*. We sent a note to the Marines near Tikrit, to tell them some of our Kurds were adamantly reporting to us that Sadaam was hiding in Tikrit.

One day, we were told that a former Iraqi officer had information about where WMD might still be located. I was tasked to drive him around to investigate, so I picked him up from my company headquarters, which was in Kirkuk, and he directed me to a certain location on the outskirts of the city. Within a few minutes of conversing via an interpreter, I discovered that the man spoke Spanish; he'd studied it at a university in Baghdad. Since I spoke a bit of Spanish, which I had learned from my Dominican wife, we were able to communicate in equally broken Spanish.

As he gave us directions, we chatted as best we could, using my interpreter frequently as our Spanish skills failed us, about the war and the buildup and everything that had taken place. He asked me if it was true that US Green Berets had to kill a family member as part of their initiation into the Green Berets. He was serious. I laughed and explained to him how silly that was. He said that one of the reasons some of the Iraqi Army units along the Green Line didn't surrender was because they thought the US Green Berets and Kurds would round them all up and kill them. He also explained that another reason some units didn't surrender was because they had no communications after the initial Shock and Awe occurred. So, since the Iraqi Army had a very centralized leadership structure, they could not surrender because they could not be communicated to in order to be *told* to surrender.

He directed us to an ordinary building on the outskirts of Kirkuk, and I walked with him in search of the supposed WMD cache. He led us into a dark chamber in the bottom of a building, but nothing was there. He told me it must have been moved along with everything else. Of course, based on his mannerisms, it seemed to me like he was just pulling a stunt to vindicate himself, perhaps to put himself in a good place after the political smoke cleared in Iraq. We brought him back to my Company HQ.

On another seemingly random occasion, we were tasked to escort some Syrian "detainees" all the way up to Mosul. Shortly thereafter, I had three blindfolded and handcuffed Syrians in the land rover headed Northwest. The Syrian men were probably in their thirties, skinny, but in decent condition, and they wore jeans and t-shirts. I had an interpreter with me, and I told them they were not allowed to talk to each other on the way. However, after about an hour, the silence was killing me, so I started asking them "what are you in for" kinds of questions. They said there was a mix up, and they didn't know why they'd been captured. However, they said they were relieved when they'd been taken into custody, because they knew the US Army would provide them a free ride out of Baghdad, which is the only reason they did not deny any accusations; they needed a ride. They said they had operated a fairly successful chocolate store in Baghdad prior to the war, and since the way they were talking and interacting seemed wildly innocent, I believed them.

I continued questioning them about their lives and what it was like when our military rolled in. They responded with the usual answer; Sadaam was a bastard, but now it's going to get messy. They also laughed about the notion that this war was "over." The relationship in the car escalated quickly, and by the time we got to Mosul several hours later I had learned a few Syrian folk songs, and these men were laughing hysterically as I tried to sing along with them. Of course, since I can't speak or sing in Arabic, I'm sure it was hilarious because I had no idea what I was singing, I was just making sounds like theirs.

We arrived at the US outpost to turn over the Syrians. I stopped the vehicle, and the Syrians said goodbye as they were taken away by some Army personnel. The chocolate makers were scared to death, and the way they were hauled away so coldly annoyed me a little. I watched as the Syrians were moved into a white building, and I hoped they walked away thinking "hey, those Americans that gave us a ride were cool." We drove back to Tuz.

A few weeks later, the conventional units ordered the Kurds to leave Kirkuk. This created a tension that almost caused a catastrophic loss of rapport with the Kurds across my entire unit, which was completely embedded with the Peshmerga all over Northern Iraq. According to the Kurds, they felt like they were being treated like criminals. My team overcame the rapport issue the way Green Berets always do, like I had in Bosnia and Kosovo; by creating the perception that there was clear separation between us and the conventional forces, and any political decisions in general.

Once the Kurds were out of Kirkuk, and some of them left Tuz, we pulled back to get ready to go home. We said our goodbyes to the Kurds over tea, packed up our weapons and equipment, and drove towards As Sulaymaniya. We drove the road of doom one last time, this time stenciling chili peppers on the road at random intervals to leave our mark. Once we got to the Kurdish headquarters, we loaded a Chinook helicopter, and flew towards either Mosul or Irbil, I don't remember which.

The helicopter took fire and banked sharply, and the machine gunner in the helicopter returned fire. I winced at the sound and head pounding concussion of the firing, closed my eyes, and asked myself painfully *"when will this end?"* I grew tense and that familiar doomsday feeling swept over me again as I pictured our helicopter getting shot down, and pictured the details of people being shredded, both of which made me yearn for our exfiltration.

After about an hour, we landed, unloaded, and I approached a warehouse-like hangar building. I was very glad to get away from that helicopter. I saw dozens of Green Berets hanging around near the hangar, all telling war stories and waiting to go home. All the other teams were jealous that my team was tasked to do both the AFO mission, *and* we were the main effort on Operation Viking Hammer, which gave us a sort of special status. Some teams never saw any combat at all, which meant that I was standing amidst a lot of unfulfilled quests. After hearing countless descriptions of varying acts of violence and incidents of gore, I became overwhelmed and decided that I didn't want to talk or hear about any of it. A feeling of claustrophobic anxiety swept over me and everything I had seen over the last three months started streaming into my head. It was as if the shield of adrenaline had suddenly disappeared. I walked away to sit on a bunk away from everyone else in the corner of the hangar.

I just laid there with my eyes closed and body completely tensed. I listened to the ringing in my ears and involuntarily re-experienced the noises and images of war that streamed through my conscience and drowned out the world around me. Suddenly, I could not stop the accumulation of visualizations that rushed through my memory, from Bosnia, Kosovo, and what I had just seen in Iraq. In my mind's eye, it was like the images of war had amassed and were attacking me. I felt like the guy in *A Clockwork Orange* with his eyelids forced open to watch horrific videos against his will, except the videos were in my own mind. I hadn't expected this new experience with real war to suddenly affect me so much.

Before I knew it we had flown across the Atlantic and landed at Peterson Air Force base in Colorado Springs. We drove a bus back to our team room at Ft Carson, unloaded our stuff, locked our guns in the arms room, said our goodbyes, and headed home. It was no different than any other day when we came back to the team room after a random day of training.

I walked through the parking lot to my truck and freaked out for a second because I no longer had a weapon in my hands. As I drove through Ft Carson I realized that I had forgotten where I lived. I felt like an alien who had just landed on another planet.

## One Green Beret

I pulled over and had to think about it for a while. I was finally able to concentrate long enough to get oriented and remember where I lived, and I headed over the I25 overpass; my ears were still ringing like crazy, and my mind was massively distracted in an indefinable way. I had no idea what I was going to say to my wife when I walked in the door. She had flown back out to Colorado with my daughter to meet me.

My mind was still pegged on primitive fears and visions of horror, and my nerves were still electrified from a severe case of permanent vigilance. So, although I wanted to go home and act like I never left, I couldn't even convince myself that I was safe.

I was overwhelmed when I saw my wife, because there were so many times I thought I might not ever see her again. My daughter looked totally different even though I had only been gone about five months. I am a very anti-emotional person, I guess I'm a typical rural Connecticut swamp Yankee, so I didn't break down and cry when we embraced. I hugged my wife and daughter and I was flooded with so many different emotions I went emotionally numb. My daughter didn't feel well, she was crying a lot, and thankfully her crying took the focus off the fact that I had just gotten home from war. Of course, my wife asked me "how was it?" and I really couldn't aggregate the enormity of what I had just experienced into a concise answer, so I said "everything went ok." My wife kept looking into my eyes, as if she was looking for something she was used to seeing and it wasn't there anymore. I didn't realize how much what I had just seen in Iraq had impacted me.

## Chapter 9
### Ft. Bragg, Special Warfare Center, 2003-2006
### Geospatial Analysis and Intelligence Instructor

Almost everything related to domestic life was permanently erased from my mind and replaced with survival instincts and continuous war memories. I could not concentrate on anything around me because of an unshakable form of distraction and anxiety. It was like I had entered another dimension; I had gone from a combat zone to sitting in my dining room in approximately 36 hours, and my ears were still ringing.

On that first day I returned from Iraq, my daughter had an ear infection. We brought her to the hospital and spent the night in the emergency room trying to calm her down. I was totally disoriented and overwhelmed by the crying, and It was impossible to listen to my wife's seemingly endless and detailed descriptions of what had happened with our daughter the whole time I was gone. I tried to block out the mental churn and anxiety, to keep images of death from diverting me from listening to what she was saying, but I was just so primitively distracted that it was impossible. When we returned from the hospital, I made sure I knew where the shotgun was because I couldn't feel safe without a weapon nearby.

After a few long and blurry days off, I went back to work and showed up in the team-room; and I was given stunning news. I was told that I had received reassignment orders to be an instructor at the Special Forces schoolhouse. I had three weeks to move my family across the country and report to Ft. Bragg, North Carolina.

My mind reeled as this additional layer of stress was appended to the turmoil of my mind; I could not believe that I had to move my family to North Carolina. We immediately put our house on the market, and hoped it would sell before we got to Bragg.

During the time I was prepping to leave for Ft Bragg, I became acquainted with my daughter again as we played on the floor in front of the fireplace. She really had no idea who I was, because I had left for Iraq when she was barely four months old. I kept running her through animal identification drills in a funny way, and she started to warm up to me after a few days. I also put her in the carrier on my chest and went for walks to show her things. I kept thinking about what her life would have been like if I had died in Iraq. This was also the first time in my adult life that I really took notice of where I lived; I never cared before, because I was always daydreaming about a glorious war in some faraway place too much to see what was right in front of me. Although I was glad to be home, it was very frustrating and difficult to concentrate on anything.

The stress of trying to sell the house and coordinating all the moving logistics was brutal and overwhelming because I just couldn't stop thinking about the war; my mind was simply not my own. I could barely do all the painful bureaucratic out-processing on base, and then I would come home to find that I was completely incompetent at anything remotely related to domestic life. Garbage day? Clean the dishes? Clean the house? Cook? Eat food at a specific time? How?

I barely slept, and when I did sleep I had nightmares. When the lights went out at night, and all was quiet except for the incessant ringing in my ears, that's when my mind would go crazy. I could not stop thinking about Viking Hammer, the hair cutting, and the relentless killing of Iraqis; I was overwhelmed by the horror that incessantly churned in my mind. The feeling of guilt, and disappointment in myself was awful. Every day when I drove home I expected to open the door and see my wife and daughter beheaded with the words Ansar Al Islam written in Arabic in their blood on the walls. Scenarios like this were *highly plausible* in my mind, and I truly expected that things like that could happen.

Most of the time I just wanted to go hide somewhere alone and think; to try and sort everything out in my head, it was as if my mind was writhing with pain that came from some indefinable source within my soul or conscience. My wife was worried and frustrated, and her consternation added another layer of stress to it all.

When the time came to actually move to North Carolina, my wife and daughter flew back to my parents' home in Connecticut again, the movers packed up our whole house, and my father flew out to Colorado so he could drive with me to Ft Bragg (I was towing my wife's car with my truck). When I saw my father at the airport, I almost broke down, because I could tell by the way he looked at me that he understood everything. My wife and daughter got on a plane, and my father and I hit the road.

About half way across the country the stress in my mind reached a tipping point, and my entire body and mind suddenly shut down. We stopped at a hotel and I slept, with monumentally realistic nightmares, for almost 24 hours straight. We continued onward, then dropped off the car at Ft Bragg, turned in the trailer, and then drove my truck all the way to Connecticut to pick up my family. After a few weeks of failed attempts at relaxation in Connecticut, my wife and daughter and I headed back to Bragg so I could sign in and find out what I'd be teaching at the US Army John F Kennedy Special Warfare Center and School, otherwise known as SWC (pronounced like "swick"), which stands for Special Warfare Center. SWC is essentially the "Green Beret University."

Before I reported to SWC, my old team Sergeant, Frank, who had been my Team Sergeant in Kosovo, contacted me. He was the senior Noncommissioned Officer at a new course called the "18F" course at SWC, referred to as the "eighteen fox" course. The 18F course was called the Special Forces Intelligence Sergeants Course (SFISC). An 18F is the intelligence specialist on a Green Beret team, sometimes called an "operations and intelligence" specialist.

This new course aspired to teach 18Fs how to leverage advanced technologies and analytics against Special Forces intelligence and Unconventional Warfare (UW) problems; a very new and paradigm shifting concept. When Frank described it to me, and then asked me if I wanted to be an instructor on the 18F committee, I said yes without hesitation. I had lost all desire to play war anymore, and that's what most of the other courses at SWC are all about, so I was thankful for the opportunity to do something different. Plus, I was excited to work for Frank again, and my wife told me all this technology stuff might be useful when I retired in 9 years. She had a good point, as usual, because the ability to run 25 miles with a hundred-pound rucksack on my back, slaughter a few people, then run back without breaking a sweat wouldn't exactly transfer well to opportunities within the civilian sector. I was a good leader, and a very driven person with a lot of creativity and a dash of college education, but I was still pretty much a dumbass with no applicable life skills at this point, other than some leadership and team building skills.

Becoming a member of the 18F committee was the beginning of a life changing intellectual journey.

My wife and I bought a small house in Hope Mills, a small town south of Ft Bragg. On the first night in our new home, someone slashed all four tires in my truck. Frank came over to help me get new tires put on. Also, someone stole my lawn mower out of the front yard while I was in the back yard. It wasn't a warm welcome. All these things added to my stress level, and the unexplainable difficulties I was having with being home from war. Within a few days I had in-processed Ft Bragg, my family was settled in, we were friends with the neighbors, and I was off to work.

Frank and I walked into the messy, wide open office area and I felt like I had just been beamed into the star trek enterprise. There were dozens of computers and computer screens everywhere, boxes of software of different kinds were all over the desks, and there were large posters on the walls with link-nodal diagrams and fancy maps with swirling colors on them. The place was dripping with technology. I walked around and shook everyone's hands, and they were surprised that I was only an E6. They were all either senior NCOs, retired senior NCOs, or retired Warrant Officers.

The other instructors taught Link Analysis, the Intelligence Cycle, data mining, and various other discrete classes on different software, analytics, and intelligence techniques; most of which I knew nothing about. Since the course was so new, the curriculum was not well defined. When each of the instructors described what they taught to me, what they said was so full of technical and software specific jargon that I had absolutely no idea whatsoever what any of them were talking about, which of course I humbly admitted.

They told me that I was going to teach something called *Geographic Information Systems* (GIS) (which I initially assumed was some kind of weapon system). I didn't know what *information* was, I didn't know what a *system* was, and I didn't know what *geography* was in relation to these things called information or systems. Someone sensed my confusion and told me it was "a program on your computer for looking at maps." They also said that supposedly it could be used for other *analytics* as well, but no one there had figured that part out yet. Of course, I didn't know what *"analytics"* were either. Most of the words they used meant nothing to me.

The Warrant Officer in charge of the 18F course was a very intense and interesting fellow. He was big, loud, and obviously quite intellectual. He acted more like the CEO of a small company than he did a Green Beret Warrant Officer. He shook my hand and told me my new mission in life was to figure out how to make a GIS do something meaningful for a Special Forces team; to make it do some of these things called "analytics," which were supposed to be "powerful" in some way. He was frustrated that no one had figured it out yet. I took this as a challenge.

About 2 weeks later, after incessantly trying to do something with this software that we had chosen to be core to the course called ArcGIS by a company called ESRI, I realized I had just encountered the single most challenging and interesting intellectual thing I have ever attempted in my life. There were literally hundreds of ways to do what seemed like an infinite number of different things with this software, and I didn't know what any of the things really were because I had zero background in any of it. I couldn't even figure out how to make this mapping software show me a map. I was also having difficulty just *using a computer* in general (I had used a laptop to run specific software for military radio systems, but I was so amateur that right-clicking was new to me). I realized very quickly that the world of technology and GIS spoke a completely different language, and I was missing major foundational knowledge. I didn't know how to think about *data*, what *tables* were, and that information and data could have all kinds of detailed problems and nuances. I knew what I wanted to do, I knew the problems I needed to solve, I knew the software was capable, but I just couldn't figure out how to actually do it; none of the vocabulary made any sense to me. I needed some training, so I went to ArcGIS training at a University in Boise, Idaho, and took a week-long beginner level class for ArcGIS.

When I arrived at ESRI training in Boise, I found myself in a small room with about ten civilians, and I was horribly underdressed. They were all talking about GIS and all the interesting things they do with it as part of their businesses. Although these civilians spoke a different language, I took notice that GIS was their *profession*. In fact, I think this was the first time in my life that I realized there were actually professions outside of the military, and that it was possible that the people that pursued these professions had *passion* about them, and that some of these professions might even actually be *exciting*. It was also a revelation to me that their passions were centered on being intelligent and analytical. I realized on the second day of the course that this software would have been excellent for managing the information we collected about the Kurds while I was on AFO, and a perfect tool for helping us figure out where to put our SF teams using some of the software's "analytics" functions.

I left Boise with a new quest. I was determined to become the best Geospatial Analyst in the world, and I was going to do something awesome for Special Forces with it. The same mentality and primitive conviction that got me through the trials of Ranger school, Green Beret training, and war, kicked in. I spent the next few months digging deeper and deeper into the possibilities of what can be done with the software. I read every ArcGIS book we had, and anything about geography and spatial analytics I could get my hands on.

I systematically examined every single tool and function that was possible in the software, and when I couldn't figure out what any particular tool did (pretty much all of them), I called ESRI's help desk immediately. I called them so often that all of the great people that worked there knew me by the sound of my voice. A lot of them liked my questions, because I was always trying to do something interesting, and I think most of them appreciated my insane, almost goofy, level of humility and drive; I knew absolutely nothing and admitted it every chance I got. It was not uncommon for me to spend several hours per day on the phone with ESRI's help desk. I experimented endlessly with different data, different map layers, different parameters for different processes, and all for different purposes. This new passion and obsession helped take my mind off the war that was continuously smoldering in my head.

Passion moves time fast, so one day I found myself massively excited because I made a breakthrough with the software; I finally accomplished an analytic technique that I had been working on and trying to understand. I figured out how to use terrain data and other layers of geographic information to give me the most suitable route between two points over rough terrain. I had figured out how Green Beret teams could use the software and data to generate an optimal route between two points automatically, such as an "escape and evasion route," based on dozens of "layers" of information like terrain and roads and tribes and threats and whatever else mattered to their route planning. It was also possible to generate probable enemy movement corridors in the same way.

I shared the concept and the workflow with the rest of the instructors, and most of them looked at me like I was crazy, or they just weren't really interested. They didn't understand why I got so excited about it, and they told me none of the students were going to understand what the hell I was talking about. Some of them were annoyed because they thought I was about to make the course too complicated. So, I made it my other mission in life to figure out how to *teach* this process in a simple way. The processes had many intricacies and formulating a method of instruction for them forced me to become even more of an expert on the subject.

I had another breakthrough in GIS when I figured out how to do a "multi-layer suitability analysis," which is a way to figure out where an optimal location for something might be, such as where bad guys are, or where an SF team should go, both over large geographic areas. Essentially, I had solved the "find a suitable location for teams to stay" problem that I'd lived during the AFO mission in Iraq. I also thought that if I had been able to use this technique in Kosovo, we may have found that UCPMB base camp more deliberately; possibly avoiding what happened at Velja Glava altogether. Although these types of analyses were fairly common in the GIS world, I was applying the concepts to Green Beret operations with relevant data. I briefed the other instructors on this new method of mine, and the Warrant Officer in charge was so enthused about what I'd done that he declared I no longer needed to think about anything else involved with running the course. He said, "just keep figuring out how to apply this stuff and we'll worry about teaching it later."

It wasn't long before I understood the majority of the core concepts behind ArcGIS and geography. The buttons and other widgets on the "user interface" became as familiar to me as Old Sarge's buttstock had been when I was a "team guy." Most of the other instructors were not very happy working as 18F instructors; most of them couldn't wait to get back to team life. Not me. I had found a new calling. I felt sorry for the other instructors because they were still dying to go find glory in Iraq or Afghanistan. It was just too complicated for me to explain to them that glory is very hard to come by in those places, and that they were sitting on a great opportunity.

Within the course of a year, I went from Green Beret gunslinger to what amounts to a geospatial research and development scientist with the focus of applying GIS technology to analytical problems for the Green Berets, simply due to obsessive determination along with a little bit of training and a lot of self-education.

Frank left and returned to the 10th Special Forces Group, and an E7 replaced him. This E7 was one of the most energetic and intellectual people I'd ever met, or seen, in my life. Archie was from 7th Special Forces Group, and he had an MBA from a university nearby. Archie looked at what I had done, and he immediately wanted to get it into the curriculum at the 18F course, as well as make it 18F doctrine.

I continued to dive deeper and deeper into GIS and analytics, and I also sat through all the other intelligence related classes in the 18F course. After I sat through all the other classes a few times, I realized that data in the intelligence world, which was a new world to me, was a very complicated mess. I saw that there wasn't just one database or system where all the data was, and intelligence professionals could just search and get back immediately useful information like I assumed. There were dozens of databases, different systems and tools to query all of them, most of them returned very inconsistent data in different formats, and there was massive duplication of the same lackluster information in all the databases. I also realized that data that was reported by Green Beret teams rarely made its way into any of the standard intelligence databases. I searched and searched, in every classified data base I had access to, for any of the reports my team and the CIA teams had reported from our AFO mission, and none of the information was anywhere that I could find. It was really a shame that all that regional knowledge we collected had disappeared.

When I first arrived at Ft. Bragg, I applied to become a Warrant Officer. I was accepted into the program, and I was given a date for when I would go to the Warrant Officer Candidate School. When I received orders to go, my wife reminded me that if I went, I would become a Warrant Officer back on an A-Team immediately, and I would be pulled out of this new and exciting world of technology and thrust back into war. Amazingly, I hadn't thought through it far enough to realize that's what would happen. She also reminded me that being a GIS professional was a good skill that I could use when I retired, and that I was once again in a position to go to college. So, she asked, *"do you really want to become a Warrant Officer and go back to war?"*

The next day I canceled my orders to Warrant Officer Candidate School.

Within a few weeks I started going to college for a bachelor's degree. A significant milestone in this "enlightenment" period of my life was my "Fundamentals of Philosophy" course at Regis University, my first course in the program.

During *Fundamentals of Philosophy* my whole world changed after about the first two weeks. I was stunned when I came to the realization that I didn't know anything about anything, and that I never actually knew anything that I thought I had. I had no idea how shallowly I had thought about everything in life, and how shortsighted and ignorant I was. Philosophy, specifically *epistemology*, completely blew my mind. I was able to clarify for myself the rough notions of relativism that I had experienced in Bosnia, Kosovo, and Iraq, and it made me capable of explicating all of my life experiences. It helped me define and disentangle the primitive thoughts I had about my war experiences, and I was able to turn my fuzzy emotions about it all into objective and conscious thoughts. I wrote many papers, to which the professor always added twenty different perspectives, all of which challenged everything. Philosophy was like getting punched in the face with self-awareness.

Philosophy also helped me perform and teach analysis. It enabled me to understand the veracity, or lack thereof, of the intelligence information I read during some of the classes we taught. I became so passionate about philosophy, that I abandoned the Information Systems degree at Regis, and instead signed up for a degree from NYIT's Online Program for English Literature. An English degree was the closest thing I could get to philosophy in an online school at the time, and Regis didn't have a philosophy degree program.

As I continuously immersed myself in education, GIS, and data, I developed a vision of a technology workflow that was designed to solve the problems I had seen during my experiences as a "team guy," and the problems I saw with information in the intelligence world. The vision consisted of Green Berets roaming the wild, possibly alongside their indigenous fighters, collecting relevant information using a simple app on a mobile device. When they returned to their basecamps or safe houses, they would be able to upload the data on their device to the map on their computer. They would all then be able to transmit their data and daily reports up to their higher headquarters. The headquarters would consolidate all the information into their master database, and everyone would be able to seamlessly and easily update their map with everyone else's reported information. I didn't realize that what I had envisioned is called a "hub and spoke software architecture." This vision became my obsession.

During this whole time, at home and sometimes at work, I desperately tried to evict the anxiety and visions of horror from my brain, but nothing was permanently working. If I wasn't consumed with my studies, music, or work, my mind was a disaster. I never slept. When I did sleep, it was because I'd reached total physical and emotional exhaustion, and I had brutal nightmares almost every time I actually did sleep. I had a recurring nightmare in which a zombie-like Iraqi soldier with no head slowly walked out of my bathroom with a knife in his hand. In the dream I couldn't move or speak or yell for help in any way no matter how hard I tried. The dead Iraqi would slowly slit my throat and I would choke on my own blood as I stared helplessly up at his tattered green uniform and headless body. He was emotionless, nameless, silent, and moved so slowly and mindlessly, and it was so realistic, that it was indescribably horrifying. My wife would wake me up and she said it sounded like I was choking.

I had another recurring nightmare that the police were after me for murder. This one was so realistic, that the residual fear from it often continued throughout the day in the form of delusions, and while I was at work I literally expected the military police to knock on the door looking for me in order to bring me to jail. I thought I was starting to develop paranoid schizophrenia because one time I ran into the woods behind the building where I worked to hide from the police and I ended up almost having a total breakdown trying with futility to delineate reality from the insanity in my head, trying to convince myself that I was not a murderer, and that none of what I was thinking was real.

I also had powerful flash backs and unstoppable thoughts; these thoughts would crescendo until I was almost at the point of explosive madness. It was like being forced to listen to white noise or the sound of a baby's wailing that slowly but incessantly increases in volume. I couldn't stop it and I eventually wanted to just scream and go insane. When this happened, I could not sit still, and I had to pace outside as if I had become claustrophobic. One time I almost crashed my truck on the way home because I flashed back while I was driving; I thought I was in a different place and time, pinned down by machine gun fire behind that stonewall on the outskirts of Sargat again, except this time that one tracer bullet *did* hit me in the head. I sweated profusely at night, and I became so tense that I actually injured muscles in my legs, jaw, and back due to bracing for the impact of a bullet or explosion as I relived Sargat and the night that we drove through minefields.

I also continued to get very sick and exhausted, like I felt that night in Sargat after securing the chemical facility. I described this mysterious sickness to my wife as "total body shutdown" because that's what it made me do. It caused me unbelievable migraines, sometimes I would vomit, and my whole body would become twitchy, feverish, and in widespread agonizing pain for seemingly no reason at all, very suddenly, at random, and the lethargy was so extreme I had to lay down wherever I was. Sometimes I pulled over on the drive home so I could lay down on the seat and wait for the bizarre pain and sickness and intense lethargy to pass enough for me to continue.

As if all this wasn't enough to deal with, I developed an eating disorder. I would binge eat while in a subconscious state of remembrance and anxiety, thinking about some war experience or some alternate endings to what really happened. I often became frantic, talking to myself out loud, while consuming massive amounts of calories. One time in one of these detached states of mind, in the 18F committee office late at night, I ate 3 boxes of small assorted potato chip bags; I had eaten over 6 thousand calories without even knowing it. The only reason I stopped is because my throat got so dry that I almost choked trying to swallow, and the choking sensation broke my trance. My wife was also very worried about me, but I was so emotionally unavailable that she didn't know the extent of what was going on in my head. Also, my neck and back injury intermittently contributed to the suffering as well, because it contributed to my lack of sleep.

One day while putting in a patio in our back yard, I plunged my shovel into the ground to dig out where the paver stones would be, and I accidentally killed a salamander. It was a beautiful creature with yellow and blue coloring. I had chopped the animal in half with the shovel. When I looked down and observed it writhing spasmodically in the throes of death, I literally fell to my knees and cried, and my heart hurt. I apologized over and over to it as images flooded my mind, and I pathetically picked it up and tried to put its two halves back together. Images of that horse on the hill in Tuz with the burnt eyes and shredded legs flashed into my mind. Then I clearly saw the concave face of that AAI fighter. The burnt entrails of the guy that had blown himself in half. The pile of burned bodies. The Peshmerga stacking bodies like cordwood. Iraqi's getting blown to bits or buried alive. The pleading expression in that Albanian guy's eyes as blood poured from his hand. That Russian soldier's head dripping brains in Kosovo. Heads piled in a well in Bosnia. These horrible images of war flooded my brain torturously, as if someone was flipping the channels on a TV as fast as they could without my ability to stop them or look away, each channel was increasingly horrible until my mind shut down.

I collapsed on to the ground and laid on my side in the dirt. I couldn't stop the thoughts; I did not have control over my own mind, and I was totally disgusted with myself – my weakness. I picked myself up off the ground and continued to dig mindlessly. These types of uncontrollable thoughts got worse, and I am ashamed to say that I contemplated suicide as the only possible way to gain control, or clear the noise, guilt, and disappointment in myself from my head. In my mind, suicide was starting to feel like the only course of action that led to a sense of control.

I also received word that one of my former teammates and a friend, who had stayed in Iraq after I left, was killed by one of the first roadside bombs in the war. People used to say we looked like brothers; it hurt badly. I kept asking myself, what did he die for? What did he *really* die for?

I knew I had to take action, because I was spiraling into complete insanity, so I went to the base clinic, and told them about all of my ailments. I saw a shrink of course, and I was diagnosed with severe PTSD, which for some reason didn't seem possible to me. I just didn't think Green Berets could get PTSD; it was massively humbling because I thought of PTSD as a sign of weakness. I was always the toughest of the tough, and this diagnosis made me wonder if I had ever really known myself for all those years, that I was not the tough guy I always thought I was. They prescribed me anti-depressants, a prescription grade sleep aid, and migraine medication.

I told them about Sargat, and that I thought I might have been poisoned, hence the reason for the "total body shutdown" I continuously felt ever since Viking Hammer. I don't think they believed me, the doctor looked at me like I was nuts (which they just got done telling me I *was*), and I was afraid that talking about it anymore would have been leaking classified information (it wouldn't have been), so I gave up on that. I started taking the sleeping pills they gave me that day, and those worked pretty well. But within a day or two I took the anti-depressant, and that made me feel completely insane. I spent a night in my closet with the door closed holding my shotgun nervously in the dark, feeling suicidal as hell, wishing someone would open the door. I never took those again. The first time I took the migraine medication I thought my heart was going to stop, so I never took those again. The sleep aid's effectiveness degraded over time until I had to take two to go to sleep...then three...then four, and finally I decided that I was growing dependent on them so I stopped those as well. After trying several other prescribed medications, I decided that these pills were all bullshit. I needed to get through this *my way*: with brute force, will, logic, and maniacal optimism.

I just kept moving forward like I always had, challenging myself internally, being positive and humble, and ultimately life at home was great. It was when I was alone and my mind was not engaged that the insanity would sweep over me. I spent the hot North Carolina summers in the pool with my daughter. I wrote and recorded my own instrumental guitar music before my daughter was born and before the war, so we danced to Joe Satriani's *Surfing with the Alien* as well as some of my own recorded tunes together for what seemed like hours. She told me beautifully random stories about princesses as she ran back and forth in her favorite green dress that she refused to take off, diving in and out of her little puffy pink chair. We set up the Barbie dolls so Ken was a hostage and the Barbies were a Special Forces team whose mission was to rescue him. On other days, all the stuffed animals were indigenous resistance fighters who the Barbies trained to overthrow the corrupt government that had imprisoned Ken for no reason. Most scenarios ended in everyone becoming friends and having tea together talking about how silly it was that they had ever been fighting in the first place, and the real cause of it all was that a small minority of them were just being dumbasses. We frequently went for "daddy day" picnics around a local pond outside Ft Bragg, threw stones into the water and looked for snakes. These were the most powerful days of my life.

Ultimately, when I look back at the pain my mind was in, and the amazing interaction I had with my daughter, I think that my daughter saved my life. She made me glad that I was alive. She made me think there was a chance I could pull through the confusion in my head, that I *needed* to pull through it, because I wanted to be there for her and see her thrive. I wanted to keep seeing her run to me and hug me every day when I walked in the door. After war, there is a noise in your head that never stops. The noise is full of screams and explosions and blood and the smell of burnt flesh and guilt and sadness and regret and endless pain and fear. It's like a background noise that steals your soul and attention away from everything in life. She helped me push that noise back and keep it at bay.

I eventually concluded that there were two paths I could take in my postwar life: go down in flames feeling sorry for myself taking a slew of counterproductive pills, or try to overcome it all by achieving fatherly, technological, and philosophical awesomeness in ways I had never thought of before. I chose the latter. For the first time since my childhood, I understood what a normal family life as a husband and father was, and I liked it. The smoke started to clear a bit over time.

The first day I stood on the podium to teach my new curriculum it was total chaos. Nothing I said made any sense to anyone in the class. My vocabulary had morphed into that of a typical technology or GIS professional. I used terms like tables and rows and shapefiles and columns and fields and databases and geometry and friction surface and probabilistic reasoning and raster and vector and overlay and all sorts of references and contexts that I didn't realize were very esoteric. The students' endless questions, and their obvious frustration with my geeky language usage, caused me to subsequently understand the material better and explain it all in a more understandable way. I beamed myself back in time, and imagined someone explaining it all to me then.

I somehow survived the first class, got a lot of feedback, most of which was negative, and I went back to the drawing board to re-imagine my instruction modules so they would be easier for the students to follow and understand the next time. I decided to teach the principles with a paper map first, and then show them how to translate the concepts to the software. The next class went very well, and most of the students were enthused about how they could apply these analysis techniques to what they were doing in Afghanistan and Iraq.

Just when I had great momentum, I was given orders to go to the Advanced Non-Commissioned Officer Course (ANCOC, typically pronounced "A-knock"), which was at Ft. Bragg. I didn't even feel like I was in the Army anymore, I'd mentally checked out, so ANCOC was like being forced back into the Army for three months.

I immediately realized, within minutes of my arrival to ANCOC, that I had become completely detached from the Army. I had been working as a geospatial data scientist, college student, and teacher for the year prior, and I was totally disconnected from the military thinking of my peers. I observed the sea of my Green Beret peers standing around telling war stories, and I confirmed very quickly that I was not who I used to be. I had changed so fast that it was like I was in a foreign environment. I had no choice but to treat ANCOC like another peacekeeping mission in order to survive it. I felt like the guy in Plato's allegory of the Cave, the one that escaped and discovered the colorful real world, and I had just walked back into the cave.

I survived all the notorious ANCOC training, like how to council troops, how to get awards situated properly on a dress uniform, I jumped out of planes and did some field exercises, and ostensibly learned about leadership. It was all *training*, and because I was fairly far along in college it became apparent to me that the NCO corps in SF would be way better served with an *education* approach to professional development. Interestingly, not only did I survive ANCOC, but somehow I actually ended up being the recipient of the *ANCOC Leadership Award*. It was humorous to me, because I just wanted to get back to my computer as fast as I could to keep learning how to answer hard questions with complex data.

After almost 2 years at the 18F course, Archie got me more involved in other facets of the course. Archie had the same level of energy that I did for technology and intellectualism, so he and I re-imagined many aspects of the course. I became heavily involved with the "graph theory" aspects of "Link Analysis" and became very familiar with those software tools and analyses. In fact, the primary instructor for Link Analysis and I worked together all the time to figure out how to create synergy between mapping software and link analysis software. I also learned more and more about the general discipline of what is called "all-source intelligence." Analytic magic and innovation abounded, and soon enough we had built a course that was renowned by all the services in Special Operations.

## One Green Beret

While creating my curriculum and learning about the business of intelligence. I could still picture myself in Bosnia, Kosovo, and Iraq, writing all those reports, and crazily putting notes on paper wall-maps with thumb tacks for reference, and it dawned on me that using a Geographic Information System like ArcGIS, I could actually put *structure* to those notes, and the report could be instantly *accessible from a digital map when you clicked on it*. I started tinkering with what is referred to in computer science as "data modeling" using ArcGIS tools, figuring out what fields needed to be in what types of layers for it to make sense and support certain reports and analytics.

One day I called the ESRI help desk to ask them how I would accomplish a custom "data entry form" for my data model, and they casually said something like

"Oh, you'd have to write code for that."

"*Write code*?"

I really wasn't sure what "write code" meant, but it sounded like another new challenge, so I again raised the bar in my mind. Since I didn't even know what "code" was, I immediately signed up for an ESRI programming course called "Programming ArcObjects with VBA" and Archie allowed me to go immediately. My mind was set on achieving my vision of a complete system, and it appeared that programming was the next necessary step to see it through. The ESRI course was amazing; I learned what code was, and more.

It wasn't long before I was writing code back at the office. I was programming, and it was the most exhilarating thing I had ever done in my life. The first time I made a "for each" loop code-block work in my debugger, and I could see real data moving through my program, I felt different than I ever had in my life. It was just as exciting to me as jumping out of a plane or charging the enemy amongst a horde of Peshmerga.

In conjunction with programming, I continued to perfect what I called "The 18F Data Model." It was a custom database model for storing different types of reports that Green Berets write, and a format for each. I also tinkered with Mobile GIS tools, GPS hand held devices, because collecting information from the field was part of my grand vision. When users used this database along with a tool called ArcPAD, it would give them dropdown menus for the report types, and other fields that made sense for each report. Eventually, I created an "end to end" solution for reporting and analysis. The first cut of my vision was done, and I made it a part of the curriculum.

In the next class, I divided the students into twenty-five different two-man teams. Each team was assigned a mobile device and an "area of responsibility" on Ft Bragg. Each team's mission was to drive around and collect certain types of information and fill out the reports on their mobile device (in the way I wish I'd been able to years prior). I told them that when they returned they would "check in" the data they collected into their computer, and then I would "check in" all the teams' data into the master database.

They all downloaded their sector "base map" onto their devices, and bustled out of the classroom. Many of them asked last minute questions, and I did the best I could to get them on their way. Some of them were very excited about it, but I was definitely the one who was most excited.

## One Green Beret

Five or six hours later the students started trickling back into their seats in the classroom, and I helped each team "check in" their information to their own workstations. They were amazed how easy it was to get the data from their device onto the map on their computer. While everyone waited for the entirety of the class to get back they happily explored the data they had collected on their own workstations. Once all the teams had arrived and everyone had "checked in" their work, I walked onto the stage at the head of the classroom and opened up my map -the "master" map- on the big screen.

Everyone stared at the big map on the giant screen in anticipation as I began to "check in" the work from *all the teams* to the master data model. This was a powerful moment for me, the other instructors, and the students. Many people had their doubts about my vision, and I didn't want to make their doubts a reality. My heart rate elevated, and I held my breath as I clicked the mouse to check in all the data. The mouse button depressed, then I released it, and I stared in anticipation at the enormous map on the screen in the front of the room.

Nothing happened.

I stared at the screen helplessly. All I could do was wish that the data would appear. I didn't breathe for so long I started to get tunnel vision. Fifty camouflaged Green Berets sitting behind computers were staring at me and murmurs started to materialize in the room. Some of them had annoyed looks on their faces, some pitied me, some were ambivalent, some laughed, and someone uttered *"oh shit."* One of the other instructors in the back yelled "try the *refresh* button!" I clicked the refresh button on the bottom of my map.

Boom.

The map on the big screen turned from empty to completely saturated with layers of all the data the students had collected. The whole class began to cheer triumphantly, and they were amazed how their collective efforts had come together. The students started saying things like "if we had this in Afghanistan…. " and "imagine if we had this in…." It was exhilarating beyond description, and I started talking about how we can start to ask the data questions for analysis. It was a success, I was vindicated, and my confidence soared.

Not long after I started teaching this new hub and spoke system and the various analysis techniques, I started receiving emails from former students that were in Afghanistan and Iraq. This was the most rewarding work I had ever done in my life.

I wondered why the whole intelligence community didn't do something like this on a larger scale. I thought, *wouldn't this make finding information and reporting information more streamlined?* For about the last year I was at the 18F course, my curriculum was solid, so I spent a lot of time in the other courses like "data mining," working on my coding skills, and thinking big thoughts about data management, data modeling, and advanced analytics.

While sitting in the other classes in the course, the ones that were more about the investigative and qualitative side of intelligence research work, I thought deeply about how decisions were made based on intelligence. Up until this point, I always thought the Intelligence folks that had provided my team intelligence support had been worthless, because they never had answers for us. However, since now I understood the challenges with intelligence data, it became clear to me *why* I never got straight answers: it was simply because there were no straight answers to be found. I pondered about the reason for this very deeply, and I tried to achieve a general framework to describe it. I decided that the reason why it was impossible to get "straight" answers from intelligence people is because they are working with data that is the result of a complex information diffusion and reduction process. I turned this concept into a small and simple theory (I try to devise a theory or hypothesis to explain to myself how everything I see fundamentally works).

Information starts with a notion of *reality*: which is the full fidelity raw form of what is happening everywhere all the time. Then there is what reporters of intelligence actually *observed* of that reality, which of course is a fraction of *reality* itself. Next there is what is *reported*, which is a fraction of what was *observed*. Then there is the information that any one person receives via *distribution*, which is again a fraction of what was *reported*, because not everyone has access to everything that is reported. Then there is *discoverable* information, which is a fraction of what is received via *distribution*. The intelligence analysts working at the bottom of this diffusion process are working with a tiny sample of skewed reality; they get a fraction of what was disseminated to them, which is a fraction of what was reported, which is a fraction of what was observed, which is a fraction of reality, and they piece together as good of a depiction of what's going on as they can with whatever data they have access to that is actually discoverable to them. To expect a concrete answer from data that goes through this kind of process is unrealistic.

Moreover, what makes matters worse are the different levels of data classification -unclassified, secret, and top secret- and the fact that most intelligence professionals tend to overclassify everything just to be safe, which further limits distribution. There is also the blanket "need to know" clause, which can be arbitrarily applied and can stovepipe any piece of information from anyone but a small group. Another critical problem is that reporters only report what they observe based on what they are *told is worthy of reporting*, so this is where subjectivity is injected, and further reduction occurs. Now consider that most organizations in the intelligence community operate their systems behind different physical IT network firewalls, which further challenges distribution, and we have a recipe for achieving a state where no one ever has all the information they might need, and therefore we can never gain an accurate nor consistent perception of reality.

At some point, my valor award from Operation Viking Hammer came through. I had been submitted for the Silver Star, but it had been downgraded to a Bronze Star with Valor device ("V" Device). My old commander, Col. Cleveland, was now a one-star General at USASOC, and he came to the classroom to pin it on me.

My parents were visiting at the time, so my wife, daughter, mother, and father came to see him pin it on me in front of the class. General Cleveland read the citation out loud, and then asked me to say a few words. The students were all speechless because before hearing the award narrative they thought I was just some anomalous nerd who had never seen any combat. After all, how could such an uppity geek like me be a real combat Green Beret? I told the whole class, much to everyone's surprise, to be careful what they wish for in terms of their own quests for war. War seems glorious until you get there, but it's not, and once you make it there your mind has a hard time leaving. I had never worn my combat patches because I was tired of people asking me about where I'd earned them and I really didn't want to talk about it, so I guess none of the students really knew I had been in Iraq or anywhere else until this award ceremony. They looked at me differently after that.

Towards the end of 2005, I decided to go to the hospital on Ft Bragg because they announced they were going to provide corrective laser eye surgery for anyone on active duty. Since I had trouble with my vision for the last few years, I was excited to get this done. When I went into the hospital for my initial screening the doctor looked at my eye topology very intensely. He then ran me through some other tests that seemed very detailed to me.

After a few minutes he informed me that I was not eligible for the eye surgery because I had a degenerative eye disease called Keratoconus, and apparently it was fairly bad in both eyes. I was stunned, as this explained why I had increasing trouble with my eyes over all those years, like when those chemlights on the landmines were so distorted that night as we attacked Tuz, and perhaps why I had such a hard time locating AAI fighters on Operation Viking Hammer. This was just one more thing that contributed to the incremental realization that my days as a Green Beret warrior really were over. This was all the more reason to focus on this new technology obsession of mine.

As I approached the three-year mark as an 18F instructor, I knew the Army was going to move me somewhere. That's how the Army works; officers have to move as much as every two years or less, and NCOs usually move every three or four years, so I could feel it coming and the anticipatory stress was rising. I wasn't surprised when, almost simultaneously with being informed of my eye disease, I was given reassignment orders to go back to Colorado to 10th Group, to be a "Team guy" again. I thought to myself...*here we go again*....I was devastated by this news.

I had come so far so fast in those three years that it pained me to even imagine losing the momentum I had with technology. Would I be able to finish my degree? Would I ever use my coding and GIS skills again? The thought of being in Iraq again literally made me sick, and it also scared me because I don't think my mind could take another round over there. Also, the notions of asking my wife to endure more time alone wondering if I would die at any minute again, and leaving my daughter fatherless, were unbearable to me. I would have to leave my daughter again, and she was still so young, if I was killed she probably wouldn't have remembered me. I contemplated declining the assignment and getting out of the Army. I actually went to several job interviews, and I could have done well as a GIS professional. This was very stressful for my wife and I, because we really didn't have control; the Army life was getting really old to us.

Around this time, Archie had all of us in the 18F committee doing a lot of collaboration with US Special Operations Command (SOCOM) in Tampa, Florida. They had created a program called the Special Operations Joint Interagency Collaboration Center (SOJICC), which was basically an analytical data crunching outfit where they were applying advanced analytics to large amounts of data to solve tough intelligence problems. Some of the analytics I'd created in the 18F course had trickled into the SOJICC so I was fairly well known there.

I had invested 15 years in the Army, and I knew that if I made it another five years I'd be eligible for a retirement pension. I decided that getting out would have been a silly financial move. So I was in a bad spot; I didn't want to move and go back to war because of my family and newfound hatred for war. I didn't want to get out because I would have wasted my chance at a pension. It was very stressful and I couldn't figure out what to do. As usual, my wife was there to help.

One day my wife asked me casually, *"how are you going to be a team guy again when you have an eye disease?"* She was right. It was obvious to her but somehow not to me. I would have been dangerous to an SF team. I actually couldn't even pass a basic Army eye exam anymore. My eyes had played tricks on me three years prior, and the degeneration had advanced since then.

I did some internal schmoozing with the people I knew at SOCOM, and with the E7 who handled assignments for the SF Branch. I landed a reassignment to USSOCOM to be the lead of the Geospatial Analysis section in the SOJICC. Today I thank my wife for always thinking more than I did about everything in life, always knowing where to point me, and I'm glad I got an eye disease, it was perfect.

We were on our way to Tampa, where my evolution became turbo charged.

# Chapter 10
## USSOCOM, 2006-2011
### Inter-agency Task Force

Archie convinced me to attend Army Jumpmaster school on my way to Tampa. I had no personal desire whatsoever to attend the course, nor any other military course of any kind, but he insisted I would never get promoted without the Jumpmaster qualification, so I agreed to go. It was 2006, and my wife and I had already bought a house in a town about 30 miles east of Tampa. The housing market was super inflated, and of course we didn't have a lot of money, so we had to keep moving east from Tampa until we could afford something.

I wasn't thinking about Jumpmaster School at all as I drove to Alabama where the course was being held; it meant absolutely nothing to me. Instead, I thought obsessively about everything I was going to do at SOCOM to make a difference there. I dreamt of technology similarly to how I used to dream of achieving glory in war years prior.

As I signed into the course, I met a Captain from the 5th SF Group who was also attending, and he asked me about my time in Iraq. We started talking about our experiences and found some common ground. We had long conversations about philosophy and God and war. We philosophized about whether or not war is an inescapable human behavior, or something that is actually possible to eradicate. He was very religious, I am not, and we had some massive conversations about religion and war that I won't forget. He kept trying to get me to go to church with him, but I just couldn't. I think we were giving each other some war therapy.

Jumpmaster school was intellectually easy but physically brutalizing. Like most Army training, it consisted of repetitive physical tasks with binary results, which was becoming more and more intolerable to the new me. The night jump was difficult for me because I had a hard time spotting the chemlights from the air because my eyes were so bad (I actually wasn't qualified to even go to jumpmaster school because of my eyesight, I kind of schmoozed my way in). On the last day of the course, we did five jumps in one day. I reinjured my back and neck badly (recall that I had injured my back just prior to going to Iraq on a parachute jump in Colorado). I could barely turn my head in any direction, and my neck and upper back muscles spasmed like crazy. It was incredibly painful.

I graduated Jumpmaster school, got a star on my Army parachutist badge, and I wished the Captain good luck in his future endeavors at war. I hope he came out of the wars ok. I drove back to Bragg the next day.

When I returned to Ft Bragg, I went to the clinic immediately due to my back injury. They eventually took some xrays, catscans, and an MRI on my back and neck. They found three bulged disks in my neck that caused pinched nerves and muscle spasms, arthritis throughout my upper back and neck, and there was significant degeneration and several small fractures. They gave me naproxen for the swelling, told me that I had no business jumping out of planes anymore, and that I should sign up for physical therapy as soon as I arrived in Tampa. I was no longer just blind and crazy, my body was also broken, which further humbled me and legitimized my new life goals. I completely out-processed Ft Bragg, and drove down to Florida to link up with my family that night.

My truck got a flat tire somewhere along a desolate stretch of interstate 95 in South Carolina during the middle of the night. I had a significant flashback while putting on the spare. I thought I needed to escape and evade imminent capture, that I was trapped behind enemy lines or something. I snapped out of the delusion when I realized I was frantically thrashing through the woods several hundred meters away from the side of the highway. I felt like a fool, and walked towards the noise of the highway under the moonlight back to my truck. I finished changing the tire, and then continued south.

Before long my family and I were settled into our house in Florida, and I was driving into MacDill Air Force Base.

I wasn't surprised when the first day at SOCOM turned into a nightmare.

I was supposed to be assigned to the SOJICC, to lead a team of Geospatial Analysts and computer programmers. However, one of the Sergeant Majors at SOCOM had other plans. To my horror, he hijacked me and assigned me to do menial administrative tasks as a "liaison officer" for one of SOCOM's subordinate units. I tried to explain to him the value that I was going to bring to the SOJICC program, but in his mind I was an enlisted Green Beret and I shouldn't be playing with computers all day.

I spent my first week at SOCOM thoroughly depressed, sitting in an office learning about this job that I dreaded the thought of doing for the next five years. I had no software to write code with, no GIS tools, no data. I felt very similar to when I thought I wouldn't be going to war with my team a few years earlier; like my world was collapsing. Luckily, there was another Sergeant Major who understood that I had developed some skills that he thought would be valuable to the SOJICC. Within a few days, thanks to this other Sergeant Major, I was rescued from administrative hell.

I met my new leader, a ranking government civilian, and he provided me an overview of the SOJICC. He explained that the SOJICC was a data crunching R&D outfit, and the array of analytical techniques and technologies he described sounded like heaven to me. I met all the people in the program, and I quickly realized I was about to start working with the smartest people I had ever known. Most of the team consisted of contractors, and they specialized in Link Analysis, Geospatial Analysis, Data Mining, programming, and other various forms of analysis and computer science; most had advanced degrees.

There was also a database that everyone kept referring to as "The SOJICC *Pit*." The Pit was many dozens of terabytes of data, and consisted of just about every type of intelligence reporting that exists. People had fear and uncertainty in their voices when they spoke of The Pit.

When I was finally granted access to the SOJICC outfit, I walked through the doors and into a giant open room filled with rows of desks that were replete with large monitors. The desks looked miniature in contrast to the giant wall of oversized screens in the front of the room. It was similar to something like a space operations center, theater, or perhaps the Star Trek Enterprise. There were maps and charts and video feeds on all the screens, and people were scurrying about collaborating with each other. As I overheard fragments of conversations - and I was ecstatic that I actually understood what they were saying - It dawned on me the first day in that big room that I was now part of the real intelligence world, and that excited me. My new civilian boss reiterated to me that he had one desire for the organization: *to innovate* (remember this was 2006, and technology was on the rise). I was issued an awesome computer, and I set up all of my GIS, programming, and link analysis tools.

Although the SOJICC was fundamentally an R&D organization, it also helped SOCOM solve real operational problems. One of the first things I did was perform a geospatial analysis related to a target in "country X." I used one of the techniques I had developed and taught as an 18F instructor to probabilistically identify a target's location based on a multitude of layers of information over a large geographic area. The maps I made in an attempt to predict the location became part of a significant planning effort, and the folks in the SOJICC thought very highly of me after this. This little project was important because it established my credibility, and it also established credibility for the SOJICC.

Credibility for the SOJICC was important, because there was a philosophical divide between the J2 intelligence section and the SOJICC section. The J2 consisted mostly of traditional intelligence analysts who generally mistrust information that is not discrete, concrete, and of some defined notion of high veracity. Conversely, the SOJICC analysts were technology savvy data scientists, supported by programmers, who aggregated large amounts of data to create broad insights using "machine learning" and other really technical approaches. The rivalry between the SOJICC and J2 was like a cold war between qualitative and quantitative analytics. Each side had their own merits, strengths, and value. I wondered why there was so much contention, and why these people couldn't get over themselves and just work together.

Within just a few weeks after my arrival, the SOJICC was subsumed into a new organization called the Inter-agency Task Force (IATF). The mission of this new IATF was to perform strategic (rather than tactical) analyses; something I was not used to, and neither was the SOJICC. This strategic focus initially scared me because I had never done strategic intelligence, but I didn't worry too much because at this point I had grown very comfortable with being uncomfortable. A very charismatic Colonel took over the IATF; he had commanded Delta Force operators in Somalia on the "Blackhawk Down" mission (retired General Scotty Miller).

Within a few days, the new strategic focus started to trickle down to my level. Since I was essentially the tech lead in the IATF, I needed a strategy. Since strategic intelligence problems are global in nature, and quantitative analysis at global scale is impossible without massive scale global data, I decided that I really needed to turn this mysterious "SOJICC Pit" into something useful that could help answer big questions. There was no other data available that covered the globe. This is when, once again, my obsessive mission focus kicked in: we had to defeat the SOJICC Pit.

The first thing I needed to do was understand what this notorious SOJICC Pit actually *was*, and why it was so feared. I talked to all the contractors who managed it, and I was a bit surprised that it was really nothing more than a giant file share. It was a multi-terabyte folder full of intelligence reports with automated processes constantly injecting reporting into it from dozens of data sources. The second thing I noticed was that none of this data was compatible with any of the GIS and Link Analysis software tools anyone had. Furthermore, I quickly realized that even if the data had been compatible, there is no way I could have rendered so much of it with the tools I had; the data was too big. The Pit consisted mostly of what is referred to as "unstructured text data." The Pit was a giant pile of hand typed qualitative reporting from different agencies, in the form of simple text files, *hundreds of millions of text files.*

I stared helplessly at the folder icon that contained terabytes of data that we couldn't use for anything. My mind reeled at the thought of wrangling this much data; the enormity of The Pit certainly was foreboding. Massive amounts of historical and streaming information were just sitting there, completely useless at this point, not even *discoverable.*

I grew to love this new strategic level mission focus. Most of the projects I had worked on while an 18F instructor and since I'd been at SOCOM were what I call "whack a mole" intelligence to support very tactical operations. Due to my past experiences in war, and my hatred for marginally successful tactical operations that are strategically irrelevant, I welcomed this new strategic focus.

As I settled into my new role, the company that had won the contract to provide personnel for my team was still filling the contractor positions for the computer programmers and geospatial analysts. The company sent down a guy from Virginia to temporarily fill the programmer slot. Although this guy was a little socially awkward, he was the keenest individual I had ever met.

I watched in awe as this guy, who had a Masters in Artificial Intelligence from MIT, wrote code like an artist with a paintbrush; solving any and every problem he encountered instantly and elegantly. He commanded the computer in a way that I wouldn't have believed was possible if I hadn't seen him do it. My envy soared as I watched him work. I realized that as a programmer I was a complete amateur. I swore to myself that day *it would only be a matter of time before I will be able to do what this guy can do.*

I picked his brain all day every day for over 4 months straight -I am sure I annoyed him- and my skills increased at least tenfold during this short time. This interaction changed my professional life forever. His name was Wes, and his tutelage catapulted my programming career into orbit. After Wes left, and I got another four programmers added to my team and we were off and running trying to exploit the data in the Pit. I planned to get a Masters degree in Philosophy or English after I finished my Bachelors, but I quickly decided that I would get a more technical degree because of this experience and how exciting this kind of computer science work was to me.

As I coded alongside my team to turn The Pit into something useful, one of the developers invented a novel technical approach. He explained that we should segment every Pit document into its individual sentences, and index them all in a database. His thought process was that since we needed to find correlation in the data, then a simple and valid way to do it was to link various items that had been written in the same sentence. Based on the way written language works, with sentences being the smallest atom of contextualizable information, this seemed like a good plan, and it became the foundation for what we started doing to wrangle The Pit.

Our code, our hand-crafted algorithms, needed to find things like places, organizations, dates, and activities inside the text of the sentences, completely automatically, and then we could claim correlation between these things, called *entities*, simply if they were in the same sentence together. For instance, if "car bomb" and "Baghdad" and "Al Qaida" were in the same sentence, then we could infer an event had occurred by combining the date of the report, the group Al Qaida, a car bomb event, and that it happened in Baghdad. We focused on discovering organizations, places, types of activity, and dates. Our algorithms needed to process *hundreds of millions* of files, and *billions* of sentences efficiently and accurately.

It didn't take me long to realize that computers can't read. The scale and enormity of the data and the problems we had to solve were staggering to me; oddly similar to the overwhelming feeling of gravity I felt that day in the Sargat valley, except I wasn't afraid of dying, I was afraid I wouldn't be smart enough to succeed.

We initially encountered problems of all shapes and sizes as we started processing the text in The Pit's report files. We had major problems with extracting dates from the documents, because there were so many types of reports. Each type of report had different date formatting from different time zones, and there were over twenty report types. I quickly learned that dates can be expressed within written language in an almost infinite number of ways and formats; our code had to account for this. We also ran into the problem of how to extract locations from the sentences. Computers cannot know which word or words in a sentence might refer to a location. We wrote very complex algorithms that utilized a database of countries, provinces, cities, and populated places, along with other indicators such as combinations of preceding verbs and nouns to infer that a word or group of words might be a reference to an actual location. We utilized "natural language processing" code libraries to identify things like parts of speech, but since the documents were in all upper case most of these methods were unreliable. Once we could decently identify locations in the sentence, we had to figure out where the locations were geographically located in the real world, automatically. This led to the problem of ambiguously named places, and managing Gazetteers that contained millions of geographic place names and name variants. Guess how many cities or towns are called San Diego in Latin America, Spain, and North America? Hundreds. How do you make a computer differentiate between Paris Texas and Paris France and Paris Hilton? I obsessively wrote, tested, and refactored code until I thought my eyes would bleed, and coaxed every ounce of creativity and intelligence that I had in my soul and brain against every problem I encountered.

I coded and coded, in several programming languages, and my team continued to battle "The Pit" for months and months, and soon we rolled out our first version of the system.

We all huddled around one guy's computer, 5 geeks stared at a screen and stood gripping the backs of chairs tightly; I was the only one wearing an Army uniform. We reviewed the last minute configuration, and grew silent when my teammate behind the computer hit the ENTER button to initialize the system.

## One Green Beret

White letters spewed incomprehensively onto the black screen when the process started and my heart rate elevated in anticipation. In my imagination the building started to shake and the lights dimmed. We all cheered triumphantly as we saw the first output of our algorithmic art start writing records into our database. One guy screamed out loud "HOLY SHIT!" when we realized we were loading over 1000 records per *second* into the database. All of the intelligence folks in the open room giggled at our excitement, and the mapping app started to get results and plot information instantly. My heart raced in a similar fashion as it had during combat, except rather than feeling the emotions of fear, anger, and doom, I now felt joyful and content. I was immensely proud of what we'd accomplished; it was all so new and exciting.

The program ran and ran without fail, and after a while we had written a billion sentences into the database and extracted over 50 million links between terrorist organizations worldwide. One of the developers on my team was an awesome web site developer, and he made an app that allowed people to search the system and see information instantly on a map. We were able to provide high level statistics over large areas of the globe about organizations and activities grouped by time intervals and locations in milliseconds. I was elated. I had never put so much intellectual effort into anything so technical before this. I couldn't stop thinking about all the other creative applications that were now possible above and beyond what we'd already done.

The guys on the team wanted me to name the system, so as a tribute to my passion for Philosophy, I simply named it "Plato."

So, we had tamed the notorious Pit, and enabled the intelligence analysts to discover global patterns of terrorist activities with a mouse click or two, and the maps our system produced were very strategically appropriate and insightful. The first version of Plato was great, but there were still problems. The location extraction process plotted things in the wrong places sometimes. Sometimes the wrong date was produced by the date parser we wrote. Sometimes there was an obscure variant to an organization or activity, so we'd miss them. Also, sometimes there were run-on sentences and we had correlated things that really didn't correlate, because some sentences changed context because they were just too big. We also had sentences that said activities or events did *not* happen somewhere, and our code couldn't pick up on the "not." I just kept coding, on a continuous mission to make progress.

Once I finished my bachelor's degree and started a Masters in Software Engineering, I learned that my team was performing something generally referred to as "text analytics." We were tackling one of the toughest problem areas in computer science at that time, and the issues we were having were very common problems in this space; problems that are impossible to completely overcome. It was usually during the intense and deeply technical design conversations my team had as we battled The Pit over the course of *years* that I came to the proud realization that I had evolved from a Green Beret to what is called a "Senior Software Engineer" in a technology segment that is now referred to as "Big Data Analytics." It felt amazing.

The Artificial Intelligence course I took at Regis (via the University of Ireland) was epic; the hardest academic work I'd ever done in my life. I had to teach myself math starting at about 6th grade level through advanced predicate calculus to survive, and I somehow accomplished this by watching instructional YouTube videos and doing random internet research at night (circa 2010). Since I never paid attention to any math in high school, I literally started at ground zero, and initially I didn't think there was any hope in passing. Somehow, through bitter perseverance and many sleepless and frustrating nights, I received an A in the class, and I walked away with a great understanding of "machine learning" and a bunch of advanced computer science concepts such as cluster analyses, classification and regression, neural networks, and more natural language processing.

Soon after our first version of Plato was released, a new Lieutenant Colonel (LTC) took over my division in the IATF. He declared that our new mission was to publish a detailed report about a very tough strategic intelligence problem every four months, and this goal became our charter. His vision was that these reports would blend qualitative and quantitative methods to deliver a holistic depiction of a complex situation, as well as a recommended course of action. I was amazed by, and grateful for, this LTC's professionalism. He ignored my rank completely (like I did), which I appreciated, and he just trusted my technical ability to get the job done (meanwhile I think most of my peer senior NCOs had developed a generally negative opinion of me).

Everyone on the new LTC's team, including myself, traveled to Northern Virginia to take a course led by a company called Booz Allen Hamilton called "Systemic Operational Design," or SOD. SOD is an analytic methodology that focuses on the power of depicting a complex situation as if it was a living mechanism, or a system.

Our first assignment was to produce a report on a particular terrorist group (X). We ran what we called a "SOD workshop," and my new LTC invited people from all over the intelligence community and academia to participate. Since Plato had already extracted X from the depths of The Pit, we were able to instantly show great breakdowns of X's activities. I cannot talk about the details of our discovery, but it was amazing to be able to discover information about X using our Plato system; I was beyond proud of our work, especially when senior staff members were amazed at how fast we could show a global strategic perspective. We worked hard to understand all the tendrils of X, and some of the major "system design" elements of how X worked came from my team. Within three months, we delivered an amazingly detailed and nuanced report (it was actually a small *book*) about X to all the Intelligence Community (IC) stakeholders that were interested. Our report challenged a lot of institutional knowledge about X and our own US policies.

Many people that read our product across the intelligence community did not agree with our analysis, and they cited the usual problems. We were missing data. We didn't have a "need to know" to access certain intelligence that would have changed the conclusions we made. We were SOCOM, not the intelligence community (IC), so most IC representatives didn't want to hear what we had to say no matter how good it might have been. There was also the problem that the SOD methodology produced a depth of understanding that led us to question our own US foreign policy behavior, and some people didn't like that. I found it interesting that all these people in the IC loved to complain about what we'd done, even though I had never seen them produce anything with so much strategic depth themselves. We had really challenged the way Intelligence is done by thinking through the consequences of every permutation of X's strategic environment. This was also my first experience working with contractors from Booz Allen Hamilton, and they made a great impression on me.

My access to the data in The Pit had exposed the enormity of the world's problems and complexity, and further validated that war can never end well. I also realized as I continuously contemplated my prior war experiences, that not only could war never *end* well, but I realized it was also impossible for war to ever *start well*. It seemed like no one in the IC agreed on much of anything. The information restrictions caused everyone to have a different perception of every situation because they were reading different material, and often organizational culture or personalities introduced bias. Moreover, there were hundreds, possibly thousands, of people in the IC working on the same things for the same reasons, but the information and data stovepipes of each organization failed to allow these teams to work together, and they often produced wildly different results or opinions. I concretized my opinion that intelligence is never black and white, my theory of information diffusion -that I previously described- and its practical implications on the Intelligence Community just don't enable it to be. I combed through The Pit project after project. I spent countless late nights writing code and papers for my Master's degree and randomly thinking big philosophical thoughts, and out of bitterness and introspection, I developed a simple theory on war.

I call it the *theory of inevitable pointlessness and/or counter-productivity*. This simple theory states that (in the modern political world) no matter what type of war-like action one decides to take, that action will eventually and inevitably become pointless and/or counterproductive. An example of this theory, specifically the counterproductive piece, is how developing and supporting the Mujahedeen in Afghanistan in the 1980s contributed to the development of Al Qaida. Another more tactical example is how we target cell leaders in extremist networks. We monitor these people until we have a good understanding of their patterns of life and their group's, then we surgically *kill* them. Of course, within milliseconds of their death a new unknown leader will arise who might be even worse, we lose situational awareness so we don't know what's going on anymore, we need to reestablish a pattern of life on a new person that we will inevitably kill which will cost a fortune, we may produce collateral damage that will bolster recruitment, and hundreds of people who knew the person we killed have sworn revenge; all examples of counter-productivity and pointlessness. Another example is bombing terrorist positions from afar with cruise missiles and drones. Inevitably, these bombs will either kill innocent people by mistake, or the bad guys will easily stage a scene *after* the strikes to make it look like they did, thus garnering anti US sentiment and bolstering legitimacy and recruitment via the media no matter what. When I examine my own experiences during Operation Viking Hammer, as I watched AAI escape into the Iranian mountains, only to find better safe haven and an improved recruiting base in the ashes of our invasion, and then watching AQI and ISIS appear a decade later, I think I have lived my own theory. In fact, the invasion of Iraq as a whole might be another great proof of this theory due to the chaos occurring throughout the region and the rise of ISIS. My operations in Kosovo also fit the theory, because our actions prompted the

Albanians to go into a latent and insipient state, and did nothing to degrade their true capability or degrade their cause.

While I was at the height of my creative technological and analytical successes, out of nowhere the Department of the Army miraculously promoted me to E8. My Sergeant Major was completely amazed, and so was I.

This promotion came with one instant problem: Again, I immediately received reassignment orders to go back to Ft Carson, Colorado. I thought... *here we go...yet again.* I only had a little more than two years left in the Army until I was eligible for retirement, and I did not want to get out of the technology business. I was also receiving great specialty medical treatment for my eyes at the University of South Florida hospital, and I was undergoing constant physical therapy for my back and neck problems. It made no sense for me to go back to 10th Group, and this turned into yet another battle against some of the Sergeant Majors, who judged my lack of desire to go back to an A-Team as seemingly treasonous. I explained that my eyes would be dangerously bad in combat, my back and neck were injured, and I was uniquely valuable here at SOCOM doing what I was doing.

I was not surprised when one of the Sergeant Majors declared me a total dirtbag right to my face. After my SOJICC leadership intervened on my behalf and in my defense, he said he'd leave me at SOCOM, but only if *I promised to retire at 20 years exactly.* Interestingly, he thought that forcing me to retire at 20 years was a form of punishment, when in fact that had always been my plan. It was all very dramatic and pointlessly stressful, and it was actually hurtful in some ways to be disrespected like that after so many years of service.

I didn't dwell on any of it; that wouldn't have helped. It all worked out because I was able to continue my Master's degree, write code, keep my family grounded, and challenge traditional intelligence methods.

I was so obsessed with learning more and more about programming, I would often stay at work until 7 or 8 at night. I was getting closer and closer to my retirement date, and the notion of getting a job in the real world had me both motivated and stressed. I knew the more skilled I became at SOCOM, the more opportunities I would have when I finally retired.

My workaholic mentality took its toll on my wife, who had expected to see a bit more of me since I wasn't a team guy or an instructor anymore. I often came home late, then I was on the computer most of the night, sometimes all night, earning my degree. She worked full time, so she had to deal with her work (teachers do a ton of afterhours work), all the work around the house, and she also had to deal with my increased level of distraction and general domestic incompetence.

Throughout this whole evolutionary time, I also still had horrific nightmares and "total body shutdown" several times per week. I had also gained about 20 pounds due to my post war binge eating habit. The headless Iraqi still sliced my throat a few nights a week in my dreams, and I had to pull over on the way home to stop the flashbacks or lethargy that overcame me sometimes. I also still had many delusional dreams and thoughts about being arrested for murder. In fact, one dream was so repetitive and realistic that I actually decided to go back in the woods behind my house to look in the side of the hill where in my dreams I had buried one of my victims, just to make sure the

One Green Beret

dream didn't really happen; I often could not tell the difference between truth and dreams. The Army issued me what they call a "P2 profile," which is essentially an official Army doctor's note, stating that I could not jump out of planes or run anymore due to my back and neck injuries.

Again, despite my problems, I frequently had lunch out in the woods behind our house with my daughter, and we'd go look at the alligators all the time in the ponds nearby. She sat on my lap and steered my truck home from the pool laughing like crazy. I always cooked her breakfast and brought her to school every day because my wife left for work so early. My life felt very complete despite my emotional war baggage because my daughter and I grew closer and closer.

Since Iraq, I realized that life is very short and can end at any second, so I decided I should try to do as many cool things as I could while I was still alive and able. You can drop dead any second for any reason: "get out there and kick ass while you can" became, and still is, my mental model.

Since I was promoted to E8, unfortunately I had to start participating in some Senior-NCO responsibilities. Most of these meetings consisted of how we would keep the command supplied with things like printing paper, how to deal with troublesome young troops, and other administrative concerns. I didn't even feel like I was in the Army anymore and what we were talking about was pure drudgery to me. Most meetings just confirmed that we, the senior enlisted folks, really didn't have the decision-making power we wished we had, and usually pointless and illogical complaining dominated the discussions. In these meetings I usually wasn't paying much attention, and in between fading off thinking about some Artificial Intelligence algorithm or some philosophical concept as a means to filter out the other NCOs' stream of cuss words and other primitive forms of discontent, I devised a hypothesis about the nature of being an NCO in the Army, or any enlisted rank for any matter. I created this theory in response to my growing frustration with having no real strategic leadership influence within the organization (because of my enlisted rank).

I call it the *decaying enlisted promotion theory*. The theory is based on one significant fact about the military rank structure: In the Army, any officer *of any officer rank* automatically outranks any enlisted person *of any enlisted rank*. This means that a 22-year-old Second Lieutenant (the lowest commissioned officer rank in the Army) with perhaps only one *hour* in the Army, *outranks* the "Sergeant Major of the Army" (the *top* enlisted person in the entire Army), who may have over 30 years in the Army. This is a military fact. In simpler terms: *all* officers (including Warrant Officers) outrank *all* enlisted.

Furthermore, to continue with the concept of *decay* in relation to this fact, I realized that if a Second Lieutenant outranks the Sergeant Major of the Army, then where does that leave an E7 or E8 in relation to a *Colonel or General*? I decided that in theory, the higher in rank an enlisted person gets, the more their influence *decays* because the officer they report to gets higher and higher with each promotion. So, in other words, mathematically speaking, each enlisted promotion behaves similarly to a decreasing negative exponent, which is often used in mathematical decaying functions. In my last two years in the Army I decided that the only purpose for the existence of enlisted rank at all was to make people feel good about their self-images as they got older, so they would stay in the Army, and so they could direct subordinate enlisted folks more formally.

While I was at SOCOM I wrote tens of thousands of lines of code. I coded so many Apps for analyzing intelligence and data mining I can't remember them all. I wrote a large collection of the core data processing algorithms for Plato, another app that aggregated statistics in an interesting way that I can't talk about, a semantic modeling tool for categorizing unstructured text on the fly, a machine learning algorithm that produced human readable assessments about an area of interest, and many more. I grew further and further detached from my NCO peers until basically they gave up on me because they thought I was too complicated, which was perfect because then I didn't have to waste my time stocking the printers with paper, and that meant that I could write more code and experiment with more advanced computer science concepts.

I continued learning and evolving and evading trouble until finally I found myself standing at the podium at my own retirement ceremony. I couldn't believe I was finally retiring when I calmly walked up onto the stage. A lieutenant Colonel gave a great speech about me. He stuck with convention and dwelled on the whole war hero theme. My daughter was an interactive part of my ceremony; like me, I think she thought the whole thing was kind of silly, probably why she was pointing at me and laughing out loud from the crowd below. I did not show much emotion as usual, and I thanked all the officers in the IATF for allowing me to do what I'd been doing for the last five years.

As I stood there on that stage, wearing a uniform for the last time I ever would, staring out at the people in the small audience, a feeling of extreme confidence swept over me. Retirement ceremonies in the military are notoriously full of emotion...lots of crying is quite typical, but I had no reason to cry like most people do. I knew exactly who I was and the military did not define me anymore. I could code in four dialects of SQL, I was a GIS and database guru, I coded fluently in three different "object oriented" programming languages and multiple scripting languages, I had only three classes left to get a master's degree, my daughter thought I was cool, and I knew how to lead software development and data science teams. A few weeks prior to my official exit, I accepted a job at Booz Allen Hamilton in the Washington DC area as a "Lead Associate" and Senior Software Engineer where I would make much better money than I did as an E8, and have a lot more real influence and impact. I felt like the world had been lifted from my shoulders as I walked down from the stage, head held high, and shook everyone's hands.

The loan on our house was over one hundred thousand dollars underwater when it was time to move to the DC area due to the housing market crash in Florida. My wife and I lost all the money we had ever managed to save in our entire lives. We packed up the house and prepared for the movers to come.

I sat on the floor in the middle of our garage, and I began to stuff twenty years' worth of military artifacts into a bag I'd never need to unpack again, which seemed unimaginable and surreal. I stuffed the North Face pants and jacket I drove into Iraq with on AFO into a box, along with my Kurdish PUK shirt and Peshmerga MC Hammer pants, a UCPMB beret, a Bosnian Serb Army uniform, and a map of Ft Bragg and Kosovo. With each item I packed, I reminisced in good ways and bad ways for a long time.

## One Green Beret

I remembered Pavle and his wife waving in the rear view mirror with Croatia as their backdrop, smiling. I saw the trust in my Bosnian Serb Sergeant friend's eyes as we toasted over rakiya and talked about how dumb the Bosnian wars were. I smiled to myself as I thought about the ostrich farmer, the mayor of Ignic Mahala, the Orašje mayor, Goran's fannypack, the Serbian Radical Party president, and the laughter of my Serbian wood worker friend. I yearned to sip some rakiya with them all again. But then I thought of the severed heads in the well, and the mass graves filled with contorted rotting bodies as I touched and packed different artifacts from Bosnia. I remembered those naked Russian Spetznaz guys running in and out of the Banya as we gasped for cool air, and getting drunk with them in Kosovo as I packed a Russian hat. I got goose bumps re-visualizing the brains falling from that Russian soldier's head, the blood dripping from that UCPMB guy's hand, and how his fearful and perplexed stare pierced my soul when I looked down at the UCPMB beret flash I was holding in my hand. I could still feel that grenade launcher's cold steel butterfly triggers on my thumbs and I remembered the smell of exploded evergreen trees and blood as I thought of Velja Glava. I tensed to the bone thinking about Operation Viking Hammer, cutting hair samples from the dead, and that poor horse on the Green Line as I felt the Peshmerga PUK uniform in my hands. I dropped my head and closed my eyes when I finally discovered those fingerless black leather gloves that I'd worn through it all, and I ran my thumbs across the stains on them; the smell of the gloves elicited memories. It took me a long time to pack up all those years of Green Beret memories; some memories are beautiful, and I will always cherish them and have pride in them, but some are conflicted and impossible to resolve.

The movers came to pick up our stuff, then we drove away, headed towards Northern Virginia and the "real world." I

One Green Beret

smiled to myself as I looked at my wife next to me, and my daughter in the back seat, because once again, I was *driving forward* into the unknown, but at least this time it was towards the land of opportunity within the greatest country in the history of mankind.

# Chapter 11
## Now

This was the story of what I call my "Quest for War," and my subsequent evolution; an evolution that never stops. At various points in this book I know I come off as negative and sometimes overconfident; but remember I was expressing how I felt at various times throughout my time in service. Those thoughts have evolved and continue to evolve – memoirs are really snapshots in time.

People often ask me if my time in the military "was worth it." I usually respond by telling them that it depends on what they mean by the word "it." In terms of character building and leadership skill development, I think it was very much worth it, but of course there were certainly alternatives. As far as seeing the world and accumulating unique and meaningful human experiences, it was extremely worth it. Being a Green Beret was awesome, a personally enriching experience like no other, that's for sure. I would do it all again in a heartbeat.

That postwar background noise, full of screaming, violent explosions, and machine gun fire, is still in my head, but I keep it at bay by occupying myself with things I'm passionate about. The headless Iraqi still walks out of my bathroom every now and then and slits my throat, and I still see, feel, touch, and cut that dead hair on those mutilated bodies and peer into those hideously burnt and unfocused eyes in my dreams from time to time. I've decided none of that will ever change and there's nothing I'll ever be able to do about it, so I don't give a damn about it and I just keep driving forward.

After I retired 9 years ago, I spent three fulfilling years with Booz Allen Hamilton, a great company for transitioning veterans. At Booz Allen my evolution continued at high speed. I learned the world of "Big Data," enterprise level software engineering, open-source software, leadership in the civilian world, and I also learned that innovation is what keeps a business alive and successful. After Booz, I worked as a Director for DigitalGlobe, an amazing company which had a former Green Beret CFO, and I had the honor of working with some of the guys who mentored me at USSOCOM. After that I was the Chief Technology Officer (CTO) of a great DC tech startup, driving big data and analytics. We ended up splitting up and selling, and I ended up back at DigitalGlobe, which is now Maxar, as a Senior Director. Very often, I feel proud to be with the amazing people that I work with, from Harvard MBAs to PhD computer scientists to enormously successful entrepreneurs, formulating business strategies and building technology implementations.

It turned out that the dynamism, passion, agility, discipline, patience, autonomy, empathy, and fearlessness required to thrive as a Green Beret are all great properties of successful business and technology leaders. For those young men out there who have that itch to do and be something special or different: stop thinking about it, put down that goddamn phone, and make it happen.

**The End**

Follow me on Quora, connect with me on LinkedIN, and look for my music on Spotify and other streaming platforms

Made in the USA
Las Vegas, NV
08 July 2024

92018477R00152